Autodesk® Inventor® 2021
Presenting Designs with Image and Animation Tools

Learning Guide

Mixed Units - 1st Edition

Authorized Publisher

ASCENT - Center for Technical Knowledge®
Autodesk® Inventor® 2021
Presenting Designs with Image and Animation Tools
Mixed Units - 1st Edition

Prepared and produced by:

ASCENT Center for Technical Knowledge
630 Peter Jefferson Parkway, Suite 175
Charlottesville, VA 22911

866-527-2368
www.ASCENTed.com

Lead Contributor: Jennifer MacMillan

ASCENT - Center for Technical Knowledge (a division of Rand Worldwide Inc.) is a leading developer of professional learning materials and knowledge products for engineering software applications. ASCENT specializes in designing targeted content that facilitates application-based learning with hands-on software experience. For over 25 years, ASCENT has helped users become more productive through tailored custom learning solutions.

We welcome any comments you may have regarding this guide, or any of our products. To contact us please email: feedback@ASCENTed.com.

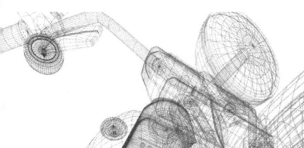

Contents

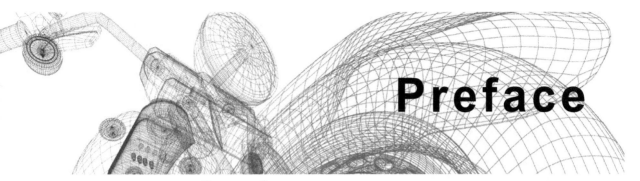

Preface

The *Autodesk® Inventor® 2021: Presenting Designs with Image and Animation Tools* learning guide teaches you tools in the Autodesk® Inventor® software that can be used to enhance how designs are presented. You begin in the modeling environment, learning how to customize visual styles, include reflections and shadows in a display, set up and control lighting, and assign material appearances.

The guide also discusses the Presentation and Inventor Studio environments. The Presentation environment enables you to create snapshot views (still images) and animations to help document an assembly and show how parts relate to each other (exploded drawing views). Inventor Studio is an alternate tool that can also be used to create realistic renderings or animations.

The topics covered in this guide are also covered in the following ASCENT guides, which include a broader range of advanced topics:

- *Autodesk® Inventor® 2021: Introduction to Solid Modeling*
- *Autodesk® Inventor® 2021: Advanced Assembly Modeling*
- *Autodesk® Inventor® 2021: Advanced Part Modeling*

Objectives

- Enhance the appearance of surfaces and edges of a model by assigning visual styles, ray tracing, reflections, shadows, and a ground plane.

- Customize and assign lighting styles to control the number, color, and intensity of light sources in a model.

- Manipulate the visual appearance of a material using the in-canvas appearance and texture tools.

- Create, assign, and edit existing appearances in the model using the Appearance Browser.

- Understand how presentation files can be used to document an assembly model.

- Create a presentation file with animations or Snapshot views.

- Publish a presentation file to create images and videos.

- Render a realistic image of a model that has had appearance, lighting, and camera customizations.
- Create a realistic animation of a model by applying parameters, constraints, and actions.
- Create a composite video by combining camera shots, animations, and transitions using the Video Producer.
- Create a custom environment for use when rendering models.

Prerequisites

- Access to the 2021.0 version of the software, to ensure compatibility with this guide. Future software updates that are released by Autodesk may include changes that are not reflected in this guide. The practices and files included with this guide are not be compatible with prior versions (e.g., 2020).
- The material assumes a mastery of Autodesk Inventor basics, as taught in *Autodesk Inventor: Introduction to Solid Modeling*.

Note on Software Setup

This guide assumes a standard installation of the software using the default preferences during installation. Lectures and practices use the standard software templates and default options for the Content Libraries.

Students and Educators Can Access Free Autodesk Software and Resources

Autodesk challenges you to get started with free educational licenses for professional software and creativity apps used by millions of architects, engineers, designers, and hobbyists today. Bring Autodesk software into your classroom, studio, or workshop to learn, teach, and explore real-world design challenges the way professionals do.

Get started today - register at the Autodesk Education Community and download one of the many Autodesk software applications available.

Visit www.autodesk.com/education/home/

Note: Free products are subject to the terms and conditions of the end-user license and services agreement that accompanies the software. The software is for personal use for education purposes and is not intended for classroom or lab use.

Lead Contributor: Jennifer MacMillan

With a dedication for engineering and education, Jennifer has spent over 20 years at ASCENT managing courseware development for various CAD products. Trained in Instructional Design, Jennifer uses her skills to develop instructor-led and web-based training products as well as knowledge profiling tools.

Jennifer has achieved the Autodesk Certified Professional certification for Inventor and is also recognized as an Autodesk Certified Instructor (ACI). She enjoys teaching the training courses that she authors and is also very skilled in providing technical support to end-users.

Jennifer holds a Bachelor of Engineering Degree as well as a Bachelor of Science in Mathematics from Dalhousie University, Nova Scotia, Canada.

Jennifer MacMillan has been the Lead Contributor for *Autodesk Inventor: Presenting Designs with Image and Animation Tools* since its initial release in 2017.

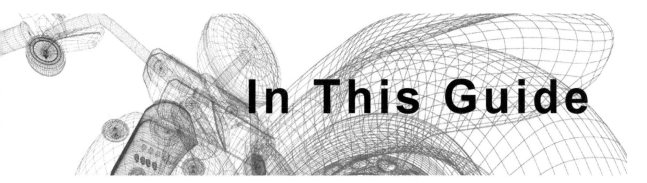

In This Guide

The following highlights the key features of this guide.

Feature	Description
Practice Files	The Practice Files page includes a link to the practice files and instructions on how to download and install them. The practice files are required to complete the practices in this guide.
Chapters	A chapter consists of the following - Learning Objectives, Instructional Content, Practices, Chapter Review Questions, and Command Summary.
	• **Learning Objectives** define the skills you can acquire by learning the content provided in the chapter.
	• **Instructional Content**, which begins right after Learning Objectives, refers to the descriptive and procedural information related to various topics. Each main topic introduces a product feature, discusses various aspects of that feature, and provides step-by-step procedures on how to use that feature. Where relevant, examples, figures, helpful hints, and notes are provided.
	• **Practice** for a topic follows the instructional content. Practices enable you to use the software to perform a hands-on review of a topic. It is required that you download the practice files (using the link found on the Practice Files page) prior to starting the first practice.
	• **Chapter Review Questions**, located close to the end of a chapter, enable you to test your knowledge of the key concepts discussed in the chapter.
	• **Command Summary** concludes a chapter. It contains a list of the software commands that are used throughout the chapter and provides information on where the command can be found in the software.

Practice Files

To download the practice files for this guide, use the following steps:

1. Type the URL *exactly as shown below* into the address bar of your Internet browser, to access the Course File Download page.

   Note: If you are using the ebook, you do not have to type the URL. Instead, you can access the page simply by clicking the URL below.

   https://www.ascented.com/getfile/id/acuminata

2. On the Course File Download page, click the **DOWNLOAD NOW** button, as shown below, to download the .ZIP file that contains the practice files.

3. Once the download is complete, unzip the file and extract its contents.

   The recommended practice files folder location is:
   C:\Autodesk Inventor 2021 Presenting Designs Practice Files

   Note: It is recommended that you do not change the location of the practice files folder. Doing so may cause errors when completing the practices.

Stay Informed!

To receive information about upcoming events, promotional offers, and complimentary webcasts, visit:

www.ASCENTed.com/updates

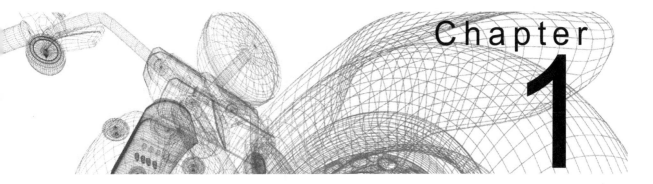

Model Display and Appearances

Modifying the display options or assigning visual appearances can help enhance the model's display for editing or presenting.

Learning Objectives in This Chapter

- Enhance the appearance of the surfaces and edges of a model by assigning visual styles, ray tracing, reflections, shadows, and a ground plane to the model.
- Customize and assign lighting styles to control the number, color, and intensity of light sources in a model.
- Manipulate the visual appearance of a material using the in-canvas appearance and texture tools.
- Create, assign, and edit existing appearances in the model using the Appearance Browser.

1.1 Display Options

In the *View* tab>Appearance panel, there are a number of options that can be used to improve the appearance of a model, as shown in Figure 1–1.

Figure 1–1

Visual Style

The *Visual Style* drop-down list contains options that can be assigned to provide model surfaces and edges with an enhanced appearance. The choice of visual style can be dependent on whether you are working on the model's design or presenting the design once it is completed. The available visual styles are shown in Figure 1–2.

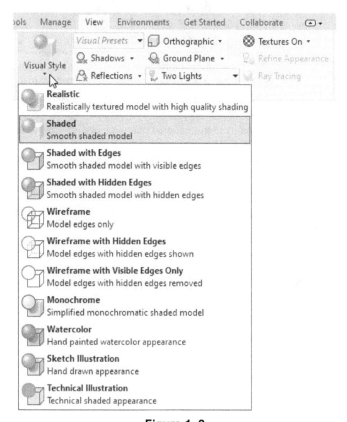

Figure 1–2

Figure 1–3 shows a few of the available visual styles.

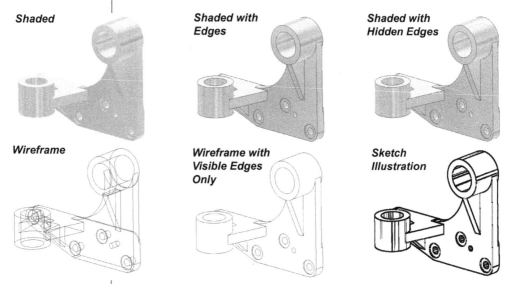

Shaded

Shaded with Edges

Shaded with Hidden Edges

Wireframe

Wireframe with Visible Edges Only

Sketch Illustration

Figure 1–3

Incorporating any of the visual styles with the remaining options on the Appearance panel (e.g., Shadows, Reflections, etc.) can substantially improve the visual appearance of your models.

Ray Tracing

The **Ray Tracing** option enables you to enhance a model's visualization results when using either the **Realistic** or **Monochrome** visual styles. Ray tracing generates images by tracing the path of light through pixels in an image to simulate the effect. This technique produces an image that is highly realistic, without having to render the model in another environment.

To enable Ray tracing, in the *View* tab>Appearance panel, click

(Ray Tracing). The Ray Tracing Quality window (shown in Figure 1–4) opens when Ray Tracing is enabled.

The render sample rates are:
Low: *4 samples/pixel*
Draft: *16 samples/pixel*
High: *64 samples/pixel*

Figure 1–4

- The Progress bar indicates the rendering percentage and time display.

- Hover the cursor over the title bar of the window to expand it to set the quality (Low, Draft, or High) of the image generation.

- Click **Save**, **Pause**, or **Disable** at the bottom of the window, as required. You can also disable the render by selecting **Ray Tracing** on the ribbon.

- While **Ray Tracing** is enabled, the Ray Tracing Quality window remains open. To optimize visual space in the graphics window, it might fade from the display. Hover the cursor over the lower right-hand corner of the graphics window to display it again.

In the examples shown in Figure 1–5, a model has been assigned the **Metal-AL-6061 (Polished)** color, and the visual styles settings have been manipulated to vary the displayed image.

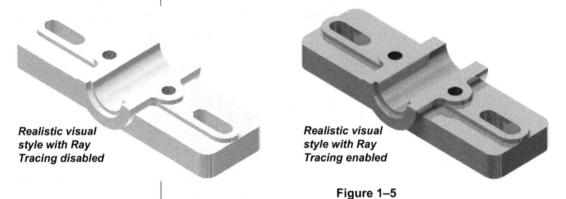

Realistic visual style with Ray Tracing disabled

Realistic visual style with Ray Tracing enabled

Figure 1–5

Ground Plane

In the Appearance panel, the 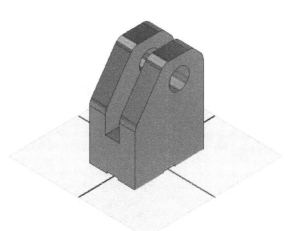 (Ground Plane) option enables you to toggle the display of a plane that represents the ground. The ground plane can be included to help represent the up direction of the model. It is also used in conjunction with shadows and reflection to set realistic visual display settings. Consider the following about the ground plane:

- The ground plane is parallel with the Origin's XZ plane.

- The ground plane is tied to the model. If you rotate the model, the ground plane rotates with it.

- When viewing the ground plane from the top, a plane with a grid is displayed. When viewing the model from beneath the plane, only the exterior outline of the plane is displayed.

- To customize the ground plane, in the *View* tab>Appearance panel, in the Ground Plane drop-down list, select **Settings**. This option enables you to relocate the X, Y, and Z locations, its appearance, grid display, and reflection settings.

- All settings for the ground plane are stored with the document only, and do not affect other models in the current session.

An example of a model with its ground plane displayed is shown in Figure 1–6.

The ground plane does not need to be displayed in order for ground shadows and reflections to be used.

Figure 1–6

Shadows

The *Shadows* drop-down list (⟶) enables you to control the shadows that are assigned in a model for enhanced model visualization. Shadows can be enabled so they display on the ground, on the object, or so that ambient shadows are used. Shadows can be enabled individually or in any combination of the three shadow types. Figure 1–7 displays a model with the various shadowing effects.

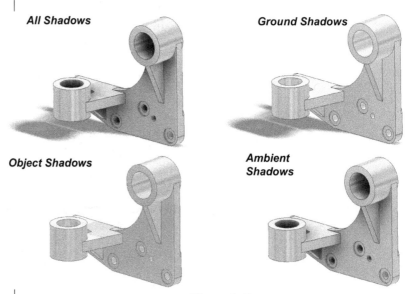

All Shadows

Ground Shadows

Object Shadows

Ambient Shadows

Figure 1–7

To customize shadow settings, in the Shadows (⟶) drop-down list, select **Settings** to access the active Lighting Style. Customize the shadow values in the *Shadows* tab for the active Lighting Style.

Reflections

Reflections can be cast on the ground plane by enabling

(Reflections) in the Appearance panel on the *View* tab. Shadows reflect the visual style that is set in the model. By changing the Z location of the ground plane, the resulting reflection is varied. The **Settings** option in the Reflection drop-down list enables you to customize the Ground Plane which affects reflections.

Note that the ground plane does not need to be displayed in order for ground reflections to be assigned in the model.

Lighting Styles

The appearance of parts can be changed by adjusting the lighting style. In a lighting style, you can control the number, color, and intensity of light sources for a file, as well as assign image-based lighting and shadows. Use the Lighting Style drop-down list (shown in Figure 1–8) to quickly assign a lighting style as an alternative to the Style and Standard Editor.

Lighting styles can be set in a part, assembly, or presentation.

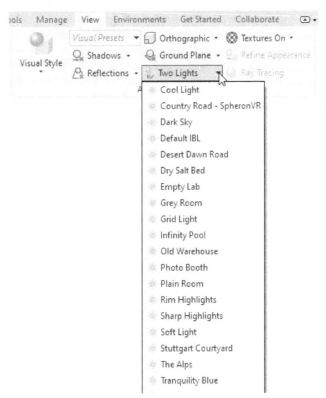

Figure 1–8

For image-based lighting styles, use the Perspective orientation to improve realism.

Many styles assign an image, as shown in the **Old Warehouse** and **Empty Lab** styles shown in Figure 1–9. Models can be positioned relative to the image to enhance model realism.

Figure 1–9

If a new lighting style is required, you can use either of the following techniques to access the Style and Standard Editor:

- In the *View* tab>Appearance panel, in the Lighting drop-down list, select **Settings**.

- In the *Manage* tab>Styles and Standards panel, click  (Styles Editor).

The Style and Standard Editor opens as shown in Figure 1–10.

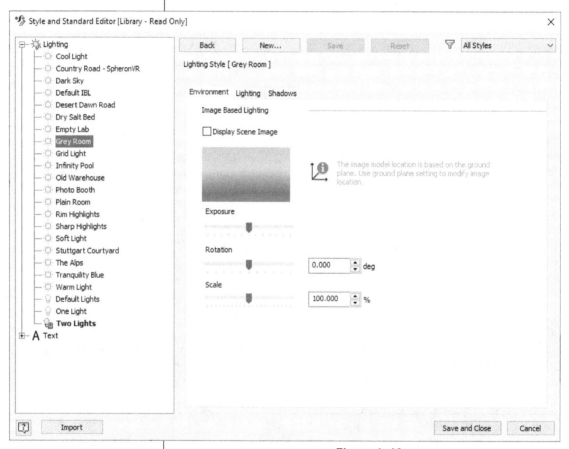

Figure 1–10

Select a lighting style to edit or create a new style. To create a new style, right-click on an existing style and select **New Style**. The selected style is copied and can be used as a starting point for the creation of the new style.

The table below describes the lighting style settings.

Tabs	Description
Environment tab	
Image Based Lighting	Set the image-based lighting effects for the active light style. This tab is only available if an image has been assigned to the lighting style. To display the image in the actual scene, select **Display Scene Image**. Without this option enabled, the image is not displayed; however, by toggling this option on and off, you can control the image-based lighting effect without losing all of the specified settings. You can also adjust its exposure, rotation, and scale.
Lighting tab	
Light# tabs	Select a light number tab to activate it for editing. Click on each tab to toggle the specific light source on or off.
Standard Light Settings	Control the horizontal/vertical position of the active light source using the sliders that surround the image of the light. You can also select the color and control the brightness of the light source. Using the two Relative movement options, you can specify that the light is fixed to the view's camera () or that the light maintains a fixed direction relative to the Viewcube ().
All Lights	Control the brightness and ambience of the light sources for all standard lights. Use the *Brightness* slider to control the light intensity and use the *Ambience* slider to set the contrast between lit and unlit areas in the scene.
Shadows tab	
Shadow Settings	Set the lighting style's shadow setting by selecting from a predefined list of shadow directions. You can also specify the shadow's density, softness, and ambient shadow intensity.

Edits you make in the dialog box are dynamically displayed on the part. You must save the edits to preserve them. Edits are saved to the active lighting style in the file.

Perspective and Orthographic Views

Traditional mechanical drawings show parts in orthographic (parallel) views, where parallel edges on the part display parallel in the drawing. Perspective views display the way that the eye sees, where parallel edges seem to converge at a vanishing point, as shown in Figure 1–11. To change to a perspective view, select the *View* tab. In the Appearance panel, expand 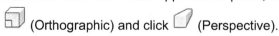 (Orthographic) and click (Perspective).

While in a perspective view, you can zoom, pan, and rotate, but the results may differ slightly than that in an Orthographic view. Refer to the "About Perspective Views" Help topic for more information on view manipulation for Perspective views.

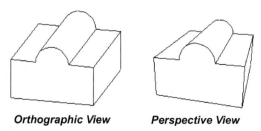

Orthographic View   **Perspective View**

Figure 1–11

The (Perspective with Ortho Faces) option enables you to view the model in perspective view while the model is in a 3D orientation and in orthographic view when in a 2D view.

1.2 Appearances

Colors and textures can be added to a model to further enhance its visualization. Color and texture are combined within the appearance definition of a material. When a material is assigned, the visual appearance specified for that material is assigned to the model. The Materials and Appearance Override drop-down lists in the Quick Access Toolbar display the current material and its appearance, as shown in Figure 1–12.

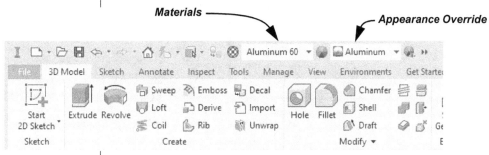

Figure 1–12

To assign a different appearance to the model while maintaining the material setting and therefore its iProperty data, select an alternate material in the Appearance Override drop-down list, as shown in Figure 1–13.

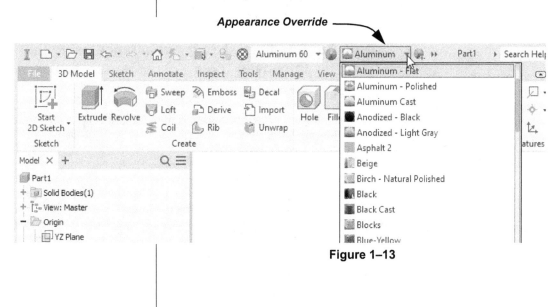

Figure 1–13

The predefined list of appearances provided in the Appearance Override drop-down list are pulled from provided libraries. By default, the Inventor Material Library is set as the active library. To switch between libraries in the drop-down list, select an alternate library name, as shown in Figure 1–14.

The default library can be set in the Project File.

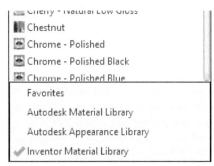

Figure 1–14

To quickly manipulate the assigned appearance, you can use the in-canvas tools.

In-Canvas Appearance and Texture Tools

The in-canvas appearance and texture tools provide you with a convenient way to change the color of an appearance or the texture mapping on the model. The tools are provided in a mini-toolbar and the icons can be used directly on the model.

How To: Edit the Existing Appearance using the In-canvas Tools

1. In the *Tools* tab>Material and Appearance panel, click

   (Adjust). The Appearance mini-toolbar opens as shown in Figure 1–15.

Figure 1–15

2. Using the model, select the appearance that is to be edited. You can select directly on the model when the cursor displays

   as the eyedropper ( ), or you can select the appearance from the Appearances drop-down list in the mini-toolbar.

- When using the cursor, if you want to edit the color of the entire model, ensure that you select the entire model.
- To change only selected faces, surfaces, bodies, or features, select them individually. Use the Select Other drop-down list to select the required option.
- Selecting the appearance in the Appearances drop-down list enables you to first edit the Appearance and then apply it to the model.

3. Select the method for defining the color.

- Defining the color as a red, green, and blue value (**RGB Values**) is the default option.
- Select the RGB Values drop-down list and select **HSL Values** to define the color with a hue, saturation, and lightness value.

4. For either the **RGB** or **HSL Values** options, use the color wheel to define its values.

- Drag the line around its perimeter to change the value.
- To refine the color, activate and drag the square node on the internal diamond shape at the center of the color wheel.
- If the appearance was selected directly from the model, it will update as you are changing the color.

5. If you selected the appearance from the drop-down list, you are required to assign it to the model. Using the cursor, now displayed as a paint can ( ), select the model or individual faces, surfaces, bodies, or features, to assign the edited appearance.

6. If the Appearance has a texture assigned to it, you can scale and rotate the texture using the and icons that display once the model or individual faces, surfaces, bodies, or features are selected.

- Hover the cursor over the icons until they are active (yellow) and then press and hold the mouse button to scale and rotate.

7. If the Appearance has a texture assigned to it, you can vary how it is mapped to the surface of the model. Expand the drop-down list and select a mapping option.

- By default, **Automatic** is used and generally provides a good representation of the texture on the model.
- Hovering the cursor over the other mapping options displays them in the model.

8. Click to complete the edit and close the mini-toolbar.

The scale and rotate icons are displayed for non-textured appearances. Manipulating these icons will not affect the overall appearance.

Once an appearance is adjusted using the in-canvas tools, a new appearance is created that has (1) appended to the end of the name. For example, if you were adjusting the Red appearance, the adjusted appearance would be called Red(1).

Appearance Browser

The Appearance Browser (shown in Figure 1–16) is used as an alternative to the Appearance Override drop-down list to assign appearances. It provides thumbnail previews to identify appearances, and can be used to create new appearances.

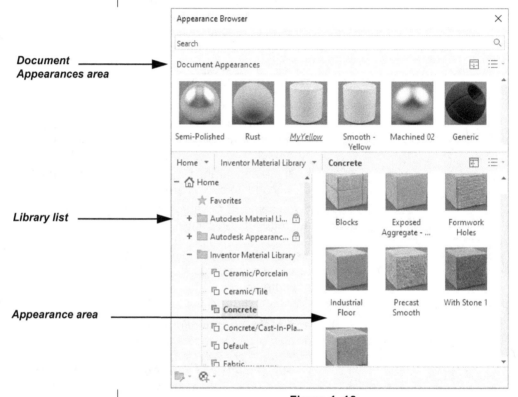

Document Appearances area —→

Library list —→

Appearance area —→

Figure 1–16

The Appearance Browser is divided into the following three areas:

- *Document Appearances* area - This area includes all appearances that have been assigned to the model.

- Library list - The library list enables you to select the libraries where you want to look for different appearances. The Favorites node enables you to quickly access any of the appearances from the three libraries that you have marked as Favorites.

- *Appearance* area - Once a library is expanded and a group type selected, its appearances are displayed in the *Appearance* area. Using this area, appearances can be added to the *Document Appearances* area for use.

Create a New Appearance

How To: Use the Appearance Browser to Create a New Appearance

1. In the *Tools* tab>Material and Appearance panel, click

   (Appearance). The Appearance Browser opens as shown in Figure 1–17. The current file only has one appearance that was assigned to it (Default) as shown in the *Document Appearances* area and the **Inventor Material Library** is selected. If an appearance override was assigned, it would also be displayed here.

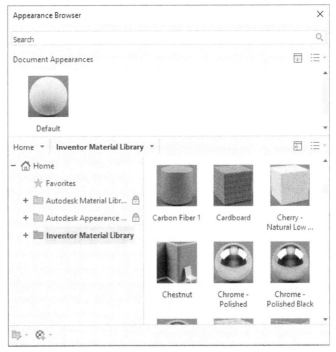

Figure 1–17

2. Right-click on an existing appearance in the *Document Appearances* area and select **Duplicate** to create its copy. The selected appearance should be one that closely resembles the settings that you want as a new appearance.

   Alternatively, click at the bottom of the Appearance Browser and select a type to start a new appearance.

3. Select the default name, *right-click on it, and select **Rename**.* Enter a new name for the appearance.

4. Right-click on the new appearance and select **Edit** to open the Appearance Editor, similar to that shown in Figure 1–18. Depending on the material type, the options and settings vary.

Figure 1–18

5. Define the appearance, as required.

- Select in the *Color* field to access the Color dialog box to select or customize a new color.

- Select in the *Image* field to import a texture for the appearance.

- Change the settings of the *Image Fade*, *Glossiness*, and *Highlights* to customize the appearance of the texture.

- Use other options in the Appearance Editor to further customize the new appearance by adding reflectivity, transparency, bump maps, self illumination, etc.

6. Click **OK** to complete the creation of the new appearance. The thumbnail image in the *Document Appearances* area updates to reflect the changes that were made in the Appearance Editor.

To edit an existing appearance, right-click on the appearance name in the *Document Appearances* area of the Appearance Browser and select **Edit**. Edit the options, as required, to reflect the required change.

Textures

Textures are files that can be added to any appearance. Bump maps enable you to further control the display of an image by assigning a bumpiness value. Texture images are assigned in the Generic node while bump maps are assigned in the Bump node. Similarly, maps can be assigned to other nodes.

To assign an image, select in the *Image* field for the node and use the Material Editor Open File to browse to and select an image.

To modify the placement of the image, right-click on the *Image* field and select **Edit Image**. The Texture Editor opens and you can refine the image's position, rotation, scale, and repeat and (in the case of a bump map) vary the amount of bumpiness.

Assign an Appearance

How To: Use the Appearance Browser to Assign an Appearance to the Model

1. In the *Tools* tab>Material and Appearance panel, click
    (Appearance).
2. To assign a new appearance, select the entire model or individual surfaces on the model, right-click on the appearance thumbnail in the *Document Appearances* area and select **Assign to Selection**.
   - To help identify what is being selected in the model, before selecting, hover the cursor over the model so that the preview displays the entire model (dashed lines) or individual surfaces (solid lines).

3. Click ˣ to close the Appearance Browser.

Alternatively, you can assign the new appearance using the Material Override drop-down list in the Quick Access Toolbar. Once assigned, the appearance is automatically added to the Document Appearances area.

Adding Appearances to the Document

How To: Use the Appearance Browser to Add a Material from a Library to the Document Appearances Area

1. In the *Tools* tab>Material and Appearance panel, click (Appearance).
2. Expand the appropriate library in the Library list.
3. Select an appearance type. The list of appearances associated with the selected type display in the *Appearance* area on the right side of the Appearance Browser.
4. Right-click an appearance and select **Add To>Document Materials** to add it to the *Document Appearances* area for use in the model.

To display the model so that any of the image's texturing settings are consistently displayed, set the *Visual Style* to **Realistic**. If not, only the color of the appearance might display on the model.

Practice 1a

Create a Lighting Style

Practice Objectives

- Create a new lighting style based on an existing style.
- Edit a lighting style to change its ambiance setting and include multiple colored lights.
- Change the lighting style that is applied to the model using the Styles and Standards Editor and the options in the Appearance panel.

In this practice, you will create a new lighting style and assign it for use with a part file. The part is shown in Figure 1–19.

Figure 1–19

Task 1 - Open a part file and create a new lighting style.

1. In the *Get Started* tab>Launch panel, click (Projects) to open the Projects dialog box. Project files identify folders that contain the required models.

2. Click **Browse**. In the *C:\Autodesk Inventor 2021 Presenting Designs Practice Files* folder, select **Presenting Designs.ipj**. Click **Open**. The Projects dialog box updates and a checkmark displays next to the new project name, indicating that it is the active project. The project file tells Autodesk Inventor where your files are stored. Click **Done**.

This project file is used for the entire learning guide.

3. Open **handle.ipt**.

4. In the *Manage* tab>Styles and Standards panel, click (Styles Editor). The Style and Standard Editor dialog box opens.

5. Expand the **Lighting** branch and select **Two Lights**.

6. Click **New**. The New Local Style dialog box opens.

7. Enter **handle** in the *Name* field and click **OK**. The handle style is now listed in the Lighting branch.

8. Double-click on **handle** in the list to activate it. The active style is bold in the list and is applied to the model.

9. Move the *Ambience* slider to increase the amount of ambient light on the screen for all lights. Note how the model updates as you move the slider.

10. Return the *Ambience* slider to approximately the middle of the scale.

11. In the *Standard Lights* area of the *Lighting* tab, ensure that the *Light 1* tab is selected and that the 💡 (yellow light bulb) icon is active. This represents the first direct light.

12. Move the vertical slider on the right side of the image to the top and the slider on the bottom to the left side to place the light.

13. Click the **Color** icon located above the *Brightness* slider. Select one of the blue colors from the color palette. Click **OK**. Note the effect on the part.

14. Select the *Light 2* tab to activate it. Ensure that the 💡 icon is enabled (yellow). Select it, if not. The blue light you created in the last step will now have less influence on the part. Change the color of the second light to red, and move the sliders to the bottom and right positions to place this light.

15. Click **Save and Close**. Note the effect on the part.

16. Rotate the part. You will see different shades and colors on the part, depending on where you placed the lights.

Task 2 - Manipulate the appearance of the model.

---

1. Select the *View* tab.

2. In the Appearance panel, note that the **handle** light style is currently active. In the Lighting Style drop-down list, select **Two Lights**. Note how the model updates to reflect the settings in this style.

3. Select some of the various options in the Visual Style drop-down list to manipulate the model's appearance. Leave the style set to **Shaded with Edges.**

4. In the Lighting Style drop-down list, select **Empty Lab**.

5. The default scale of the model relative to the image is incorrect. In the Lighting Style drop-down list, select **Settings**. In the *Image Based Lighting* area in the *Environment* tab, reduce the *Scale* to approximately **15%**. Click **Save and Close**.

6. In the Orthographic drop-down list, select **Perspective** to obtain a more realistic image.

7. Zoom in and orient the model. The **Shaded with Edges** visual style is not very realistic for product presentation. Change the visual style to **Realistic**.

8. Select a darker color in the Appearance Override drop-down list in the Quick Access Toolbar, shown in Figure 1–20.

Appearance Override list

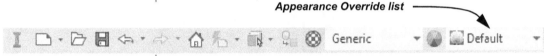

Figure 1–20

9. The model should display similar to that shown in Figure 1–21.

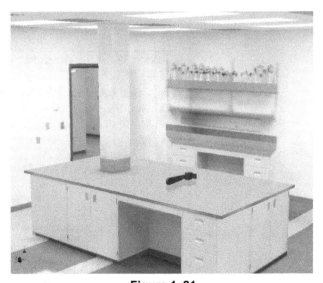

Figure 1–21

10. Save the part and close the window.

Practice 1b

Working with Appearances

Practice Objectives

- Override the visual appearance of a material.
- Create, edit, and assign appearances to a model using the Appearance Browser and the Appearance Override drop-down list.

In this practice, you will assign a material to a model and then override its visual appearance. You will apply appearances to the entire model as well as individual surfaces. The final model is shown in Figure 1–22.

Figure 1–22

Task 1 - Open a model and assign a material.

1. Open **bearing_journal.ipt**. The part is currently assigned the Generic material and visual appearance, as shown in the Material and Appearance Override drop-down lists in the Quick Access Toolbar in Figure 1–23.

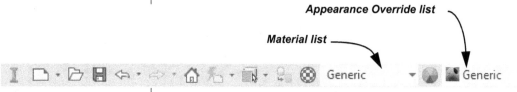

Appearance Override list

Material list

Figure 1–23

2. In the Quick Access Toolbar, in the Material drop-down list, set the material to **Stainless Steel**. The visual appearance is set as Semi-Polished which is the default setting for the Stainless Steel material. The model displays as shown in Figure 1–24.

The model's color is now Semi-Polished

Figure 1–24

Task 2 - Assign and new visual appearance and edit it.

1. In the Quick Access Toolbar, in the Appearance Override drop-down list, set the color to **Yellow**. The visual appearance of the model changes to Yellow, as shown in Figure 1–25, but the material remains Stainless Steel.

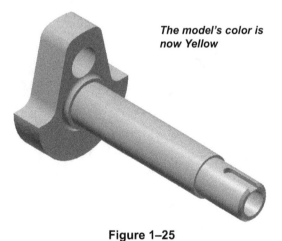

The model's color is now Yellow

Figure 1–25

2. In the *Tools* tab>Material and Appearance panel, click

   (Adjust) to open the appearance mini-toolbar.

3. Hold <Ctrl> and select the two surfaces shown in Figure 1–26.

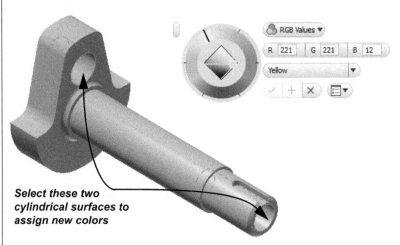

Select these two cylindrical surfaces to assign new colors

Figure 1–26

4. Maintain the RGB Values setting and use the color wheel to define the values. Drag the line around its perimeter to change the value to red. Because the surfaces were preselected, the surfaces update as you change the RGB value.

5. Click ✓ to complete the change and close the mini-toolbar. The model should display similar to that shown in Figure 1–27.

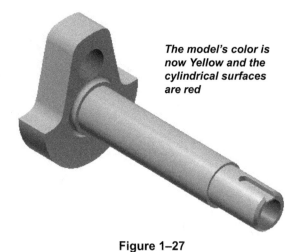

The model's color is now Yellow and the cylindrical surfaces are red

Figure 1–27

6. In the Appearance Override drop-down list, select **Rust**. The model should display similar to that shown in Figure 1–28. Note that the surface overrides on the internal surfaces that were changed to red are maintained and the Rust appearance is applied to the rest of the model. The Rust appearance was created using a texture image.

The model is now displayed as Rust and the cylindrical surfaces are still red

Figure 1–28

7. In the *Tools* tab>Material and Appearance panel, click

   (Adjust) to open the appearance mini-toolbar.

8. Hover the cursor over the model so that its entire boundary is highlighted in dashed red lines and click to select the model. If required, use the Select Other drop-down list to select the solid in order to highlight all the geometry. This enables you to edit the Rust appearance on the entire model.

9. Try and change the color of the appearance. Note how it does not change because this appearance is using a texture image.

10. Click to open the drop-down list and roll the cursor over each of the mapping options. By default, **Automatic** is used and it provides a good representation of the rust texture on the model. Depending on the surface and model shapes being assigned a textured appearance the other options might provide better representations.

11. Hover the mouse over the icon until the cursor changes to the icon. This indicates that you can now scale the texture. Drag the cursor to scale the texture.

12. Hover the cursor over the ⌀ icon until the cursor changes to the ↻ icon indicating that you can now rotate the texture. Drag the cursor to rotate the texture.

13. Click ✕ to cancel the edit and close the mini-toolbar. The original texture scale and rotation is maintained.

Task 3 - Create a new appearance and assign it to the model.

1. In the *Tools* tab>Material and Appearance panel, click (Appearance) to open the Appearance Browser.

   Alternatively, you can also click 🔘 in the Quick Access Toolbar. The Appearance Browser displays as shown in Figure 1–29.

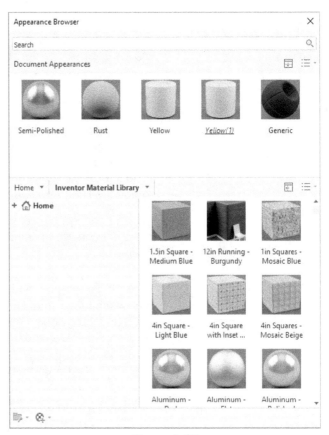

Figure 1–29

Note that there are currently five appearances listed in the *Document Appearances* area. These correspond to all of the appearances that you have assigned to the model. **Generic** was the appearance that was set when the file was opened, **Semi-Polished** was used when the material was set to Stainless Steel, **Yellow** was used to override the visual appearance of the Stainless Steel Material, and **Yellow(1)** represents the edits that were made using the mini-toolbar to create the red color. Finally, **Rust** was the final override material that was used. Only appearances that have been used in the model are shown here.

2. Right-click on **Yellow(1)** and select **Rename**. Enter **MyRed** as the new name.

3. Right-click on **Generic** and select **Duplicate**. This creates a copy of the Generic appearance that you can use it as the base for a new appearance.

4. Right-click on **Generic(1)** and select **Rename**. Enter **MyColor** as the new name for the duplicated appearance.

5. Double-click on **MyColor** to open the Appearance Editor.

6. Select in the *Color* field and assign a new color to the appearance using the Color dialog box. Increase the *Glossiness* value and change the *Highlights* to **Metallic**. Additional settings can be made using other nodes in the Appearance Editor to further customize the appearance.

7. Click **OK** to complete the edit and close the Appearance Editor.

8. Hover the cursor over the model so that its entire boundary is highlighted in dashed lines and click to select the model.

9. In the Appearance Browser, right-click on **MyColor** and select **Assign to Selection** to assign the new appearance to the model. Note that the red surface overrides are still maintained.

10. Click ✕ to close the Appearance Browser.

Task 4 - Clear appearance overrides.

1. In the *Tools* tab>Material and Appearance panel, click (Clear) to open the mini-toolbar.

2. Press and hold <Ctrl> and select the two surfaces that were assigned the **MyRed** appearance.

3. Click to clear the appearance override on these surfaces. Note that the entire model now has the **MyColor** appearance assigned.

4. In the *Tools* tab>Material and Appearance panel, click (Clear) to open the mini-toolbar again.

5. Click **Select All** in mini-toolbar and click to clear all overrides in the model. This returns the visual appearance back to Semi-Polished, which was assigned with the Stainless Steel material.

Task 5 - Add an appearance from the Inventor Material Library to the model.

1. In the *Tools* tab>Material and Appearance panel, click

    (Appearance) to open the Appearance Browser.

2. In the (Home) drop-down list, select **Inventor Material Library** to display of materials in this library. You can also expand the **Home** node and select **Inventor Material Library**.

3. Expand the **Inventor Material Library** drop-down list. Select **Metal/Steel** to display the list of appearances in the Metal/Steel category.

4. Right-click the **Machined 02** appearance and select **Add to>Document Materials**.

5. Select the model and assign the **Machined 02** appearance to the selection.

6. Close the Appearance Browser. The model updates as shown in Figure 1–30.

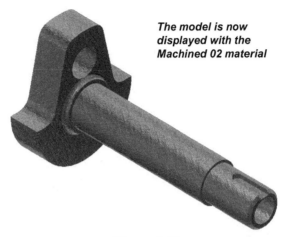

The model is now displayed with the Machined 02 material

Figure 1–30

The additional material libraries can also be expanded and used to access other appearances. By default, their appearances are not listed in the appearance override drop-down list so they must be added through the Appearance Browser.

The appearance could also have been assigned by selecting it and using the Appearance Override drop-down list to select the Machined 02 appearance. In this case, once selected it would have been assigned and added to the *Document Appearances* area. This is an alternative method to adding materials using the Appearance Browser. The benefit of the Appearance Browser is that you can review the thumbnail images and copy existing materials to use as a base for new appearances.

7. Save the part and close the window.

Chapter Review Questions

1. Which of the following Appearance tools are available when the Visual Style for the model is set as **Shaded**? (Select all that apply.)

   a. Shadows

   b. Reflections

   c. Lights

   d. Ground Plane

   e. Ray Tracing

2. The ground plane must be enabled (displayed) for the shadows and ground reflections to be visible in the model.

   a. True

   b. False

3. Which of the following statements are true regarding lighting styles. (Select all that apply.)

   a. An Image-based lighting style enables you to use a predefined background image in the style.

   b. Multiple standard lights can be combined in a single lighting style.

   c. Multiple lighting styles can be applied at one time.

   d. Shadow settings are controlled in a lighting style.

4. The following icons display when working with the in-canvas appearance and texture tool. Which icon enables you to scale a texture in a material?

   a.

   b.

   c.

   d.

5. Which of the following statements are true regarding the Appearance Browser dialog box shown in Figure 1–31? (Select all that apply.)

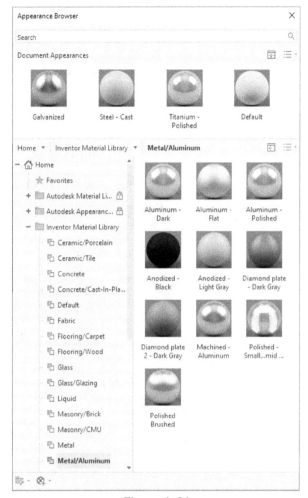

Figure 1–31

a. Four appearances have been applied to the model.

b. The Favorites list is currently being displayed in the *Appearance* area.

c. The Metal/Aluminum category in the Inventor Material Library is currently active.

d. The Aluminum - Dark material is the currently assigned material to the model.

Command Summary

Button	Command	Location
	Adjust (color)	• **Ribbon:** *Tools* tab>Appearance panel
	Appearance (Browser)	• **Ribbon:** *Tools* tab>Appearance panel
N/A	**Appearance Override**	• **Quick Access Toolbar** • **Appearance Browser**
	Clear (color)	• **Ribbon:** *Tools* tab>Appearance panel
	Ground Plane	• **Ribbon:** *View* tab>Appearance panel
N/A	**Lighting Styles**	• **Ribbon:** *View* tab>Appearance panel
	Orthographic	• **Ribbon:** *View* tab>Appearance panel
	Perspective	• **Ribbon:** *View* tab>Appearance panel
	Perspective with Ortho Faces	• **Ribbon:** *View* tab>Appearance panel
	Ray Tracing	• **Ribbon:** *View* tab>Appearance panel
	Reflections	• **Ribbon:** *View* tab>Appearance panel
	Shadows	• **Ribbon:** *View* tab>Appearance panel
	Styles Editor (lighting)	• **Ribbon:** *Manage* tab>Styles and Standards panel
	Visual Style	• **Ribbon:** *View* tab>Appearance panel

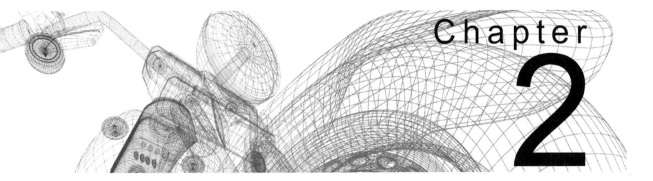

Chapter 2

Presentation Files

The presentation tools available in the Autodesk® Inventor® software enable you to create Snapshot views and animations to help document an assembly. A presentation file can be used to indicate how parts relate to each other and create an exploded view for a drawing. Animating the exploded view of the assembly enables you to further show how components fit together in the assembly.

Learning Objectives in This Chapter

- Understand how presentation files can be used to document an assembly model.
- Create a presentation file with an animation of how an assembly is to be assembled.
- Create a presentation file with Snapshot views that can be used in drawing views.
- Publish a presentation file to create images and videos.

2.1 Creating Presentations

To create an exploded view of an assembly, you must use a presentation file. In a presentation file, you can move or rotate the components relative to one another and add trails to indicate how they relate in the assembly. This can be stored as an animation or as static images. An exploded view of an assembly is shown in Figure 2–1.

If a component dimension is modified or if a component is removed or added in the assembly, the presentation file updates to incorporate the changes.

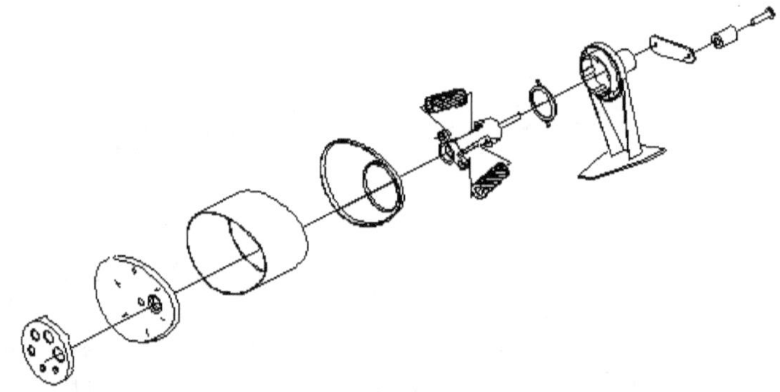

Figure 2–1

The first step in creating a presentation file is to start a new file based on a Presentation template (.IPN). To access the presentation templates, you can use any of the following:

- Click (New) in the Launch panel, the Quick Access toolbar, or in the **File** menu. Select an *.IPN template in the Create New File dialog box and click **Create**. You might need to scroll down in the list to locate this template.

To verify the default presentation template in the My Home tab, click

⚙ (Configure Default Templates) and review the settings in the Configure Default Template dialog box.

- Click (Presentation) in the *My Home* tab to create a new file with the default template.

- In an open assembly model, right-click on the assembly name at the top of the Model Browser and select **Create Presentation**. Once selected, you will be prompted for the template to be used.

Once the presentation file is created, the Presentation environment displays and you are immediately prompted to select a model for the first scene. Using the Insert dialog box, you can navigate to and open the model that will be used in the presentation. The *Presentation* tab becomes the active tab and the interface includes a Model Browser, Snapshot Views browser, and the Storyboard panel, as shown in Figure 2–2.

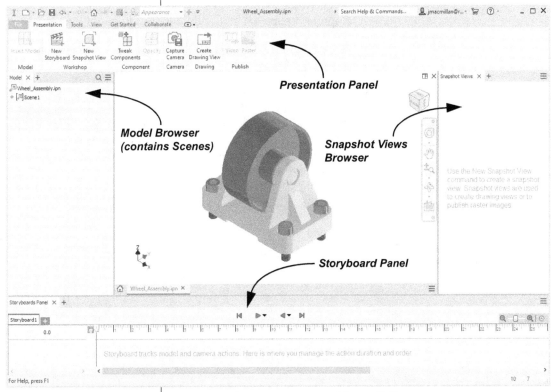

Figure 2–2

A presentation file is automatically created with an initial scene called **Scene1**.

- A file can consist of multiple scenes, all of which are independent and can reference different source models. To create additional scenes, right-click at the top of the Model Browser and select **Create Scene**.

- The model inserted in the last scene is listed at the top of the Model Browser; however, each scene contains the model that was initially assigned to it.

- Each scene can contain Snapshot views and storyboards.

Hint: Inserting Models

When selecting the model to be inserted into a scene, you can click **Options** to open the File Open Options dialog box, which enables you to:

- Insert an associative or non-associative version of a Design View Representation. If the **Associative** option is disabled on insertion, any changes in the selected Design View Representation will not update in the presentation file.

- Insert a specific Positional Representation of the model.

- Insert a specific Level of Detail Representation of the model.

If the representation of the model needs to be changed after it has been added to the scene, right-click the **Scene** node in the Model Browser and select **Representations**. You will be presented with the same File Open Options dialog box and can change the representation that is used.

2.2 Storyboards

The Storyboard panel at the bottom of the graphics window contains the list of storyboards that exist in a Presentation file. Each storyboard is included on its own tab. A storyboard can be used for the following:

Snapshot views can be created at specific points along the timeline. This is discussed further in the next topic.

- Creating an animation of the model that records component movements (i.e., assembly/disassembly).

- Creating actions to represent changes in component visibility and opacity at specific times in an animation.

- Capturing changes in camera position at specific times in an animation.

Figure 2–3 shows the components of the Storyboard panel used to create and play animations.

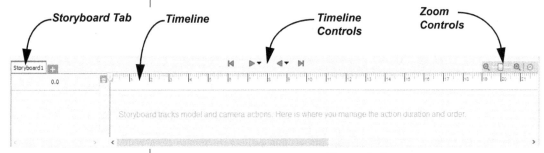

Figure 2–3

When a presentation file is created, a single storyboard is included. Additional storyboards can be included, as required. Storyboards can be independent of one another or they can work in combination with one another.

How To: Create a Storyboard

1. Activate the scene to which the storyboard will be added by double-clicking the scene name in the Model Browser.

2. In the Presentation tab>Workshop panel, click ![icon] (New Storyboard). Alternatively, in the Storyboard panel at the bottom of the graphics window, click ![icon] adjacent to the Storyboard tabs.

3. Select the *Storyboard Type* in the New Storyboard dialog box, as shown in Figure 2–4.

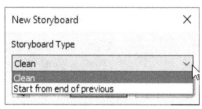

Figure 2–4

- **Clean:** Creates a new storyboard that uses the default appearance and camera settings for the active scene.
- **Start from end of previous:** Creates a new storyboard that is started from the end of another storyboard. The component positions, visibility, opacity, and camera settings from the previous storyboard is used as the starting point for the new one.

4. Click **OK**.

Hint: Storyboard Panel Customization

The Storyboard panel can be customized as follows:

- Click ⊙ or ⊙ in the panel to expand or compress it.

- Click and drag the panel titlebar to undock it. To redock it, drag its titlebar back into position at the bottom of the graphics window.

- Use ⊖ ▢ ⊕ to zoom in or out on the timeline's scale.

Animations

An animation consists of movements that are applied to selected components in the assembly. The movements are called *Tweaks* and can be linear and rotational and are set to run over a timed period (duration).

How To: Add a Tweak

1. Drag the playhead ( ) for the timeline to the required location.

2. In the *Presentation* tab>Component panel, click (Tweak Components). Alternatively, right-click and select **Tweak Components**. The mini-toolbar opens.

3. In the Model Type drop-down list (shown in Figure 2–5), select whether a **Part** or **Component** will be tweaked. Use **Components** to select subassemblies.

Model Type ➡️
drop-down list

Figure 2–5

4. Select a component or multiple components to be tweaked.
   - Press and hold <Ctrl> and select components in the graphics window or from the expanded model list in the **Scene** node of the Model Browser to select multiple components.
   - Press and hold <Shift> to select a range of components in the Model Browser.
   - Select individual components or use a window selection technique to select components in the graphics window.
   - To clear a selected component, press and hold <Ctrl> and select it a second time.
   - All selected components are highlighted in blue.

5. Select the type of tweak. A triad will display on a face of the first selected component, similar to that shown in Figure 2–6 for a Move Tweak.
   - Click **Move** in the mini-toolbar to move the selected component linearly in the X, Y, or Z directions.
   - Click **Rotate** in the mini-toolbar to rotate the selected components in the XY, YZ, or XZ planes.

Figure 2–6

If multiple components have been selected for a Tweak, the triad displays on the first object that was selected.

The default direction on the triad is gold.

6. (Optional) Reposition the triad if it does not meet the orientation requirements for the tweak.

- Click **Locate** in the mini-toolbar. Hover the cursor over a new face reference and once the required control point on the face highlights, click to relocate the triad.
- Use **Local** or **World** in the mini-toolbar to orient the triad relative to the component's coordinate system or the assembly coordinate system, respectively.

7. Select the control handle on a triad and drag it to define the tweak, as shown in Figure 2–7. Alternatively, enter a specific value tweak's entry field.

- Select an X, Y, or Z arrowhead to move linearly.
- Select a XY, YZ, or XZ plane to move in a plane.
- Select a rotation handle to rotate about the X, Y, or Z.

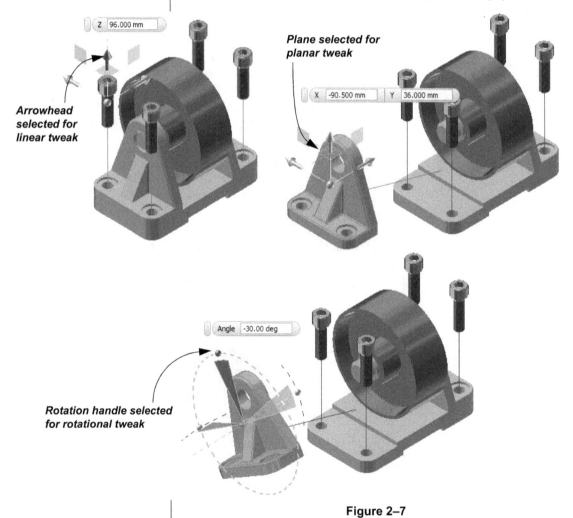

Figure 2–7

8. (Optional) Use the options in the *Trail* area of the mini-toolbar (shown in Figure 2–8) to control how the trail will be created.

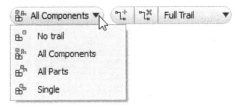

Figure 2–8

- In the drop-down list, select an option to add trails to all components in an assembly or subassembly (**All Components**) and all parts and a single trail for subassemblies (**All Parts**), a single trail for each group of selected components (**Single**), or no trail at all (**No Trails**).

- Select **Full Trail** to selectively remove or keep an entire trial or select **Trail Segment** to manipulate segments of the trail.

9. Continue to select additional triad handles to fully define the tweak or select additional components. Multiple combinations of handles and tweak types can be included.

10. Enter the **Duration** value for the tweak. The tweak will begin where the playhead was positioned and will run for the duration.

11. Complete the tweak operation:

- Click ✓ to complete the tweak.

- Click ✕ to cancel the operation.

Tweaks are listed in the Storyboard panel and Model Browser as shown in Figure 2–9. In this example, multiple tweaks with trails were created.

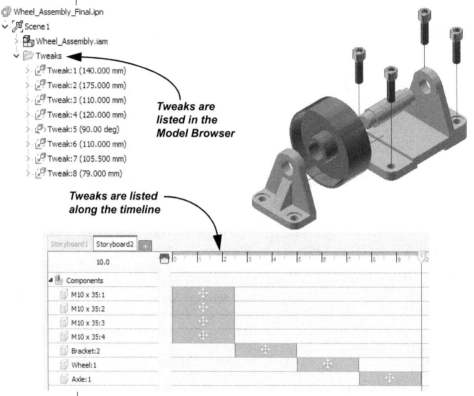

Figure 2–9

- In the Model Browser, the icons show whether the tweak is linear ( ) or rotational ( ).

- In the Storyboard panel, the symbols used to identify the duration of the tweak indicates if it is linear or planar ( ), rotational ( ),or a combination of both ( ).

Repositioning/Moving Tweaks

A tweak's timeline entry can be dragged to reposition it on the timeline. To move multiple tweaks at once, press and hold <Ctrl> to select them prior to moving. The *Duration* of the tweaks can be changed by dragging its endline to the appropriate time.

Editing Tweaks

An existing tweak can be modified in any of the following ways:

New translational or rotational movements cannot be added to an existing tweak. A new tweak must be added.

- Change the translational or rotational values initially assigned to the tweak.

- Change the duration of the tweak.

- Control the visibility of the trail lines for a tweak.

How To: Edit a Tweak's values

1. Activate the **Edit Tweak** command.
   - In the timeline, right-click a tweak's symbol and select **Edit Tweak**.
   - In the graphic window, right-click a trail line that belongs to the tweak and select **Edit Tweak**.
   - In the Model Browser, expand the *Tweaks* folder, right-click a tweak, and select **Edit Tweak**.
   - In the Model Browser, expand the *Tweaks* folder, select a tweak, and enter a new tweak value in the entry field.
   - Alternatively, double-click on the Tweak name or trail line to edit it.

2. Use the Tweak mini-toolbar to change the properties of the tweak.
   - Enter new values for the defined movements.
   - Press and hold <Ctrl> to add or remove components participating in the tweak.
   - Use the **Trail Line** options on the mini-toolbar to edit them.
   - Note that the duration cannot be edited using **Edit Tweak**.

3. Complete the edit:

   - Click ✓ to complete the edit.

   - Click ✕ to cancel the operation.

The Tweaks listed in the Model Browser are context sensitive. When in an animation storyboard, the tweaks belonging to the storyboard display. When editing a Snapshot View, only its tweaks display.

How To: Edit the Duration of a Tweak

1. In the timeline, right-click a tweak's symbol and select **Edit Time**. Alternatively, double-click on the Tweak symbol in the timeline.
2. Enter a new *Start*, *End* time, or *Duration* for the tweak in the mini-toolbar, as shown in Figure 2–10.

Figure 2–10

You can select multiple tweaks and edit their duration at the same time.

3. Complete the edit:

   - Click ✓ to complete the edit.

   - Click ✕ to cancel the operation.

Trail Visibility

Tweaks that contain trail lines can be manipulated once they are created to clear their visibility.

It is a recommended best practice to add trail lines during tweak creation and hide them, as required, after the fact.

- In the graphic window, right-click a trail line and select **Hide Trail Segment**, as shown in Figure 2–11. Using this method you can clear the trail segment for the individually selected trail line using the **Current** option or clear all trail lines in the group using the **Group** option.

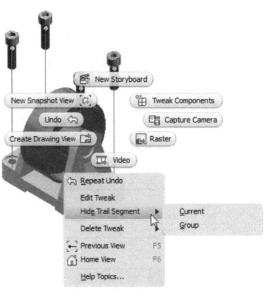

Figure 2–11

- In the Model Browser, expand the *Tweaks* folder, right-click a tweak or its component and select **Hide Trails** or **Hide Trail Segment**, as shown in Figure 2–12. By accessing the command at the Tweak level, you control all trails in the group. By accessing it at the component level you can specify it the trail for the current component (**Current**) or all components in the group are to be cleared (**Group**).

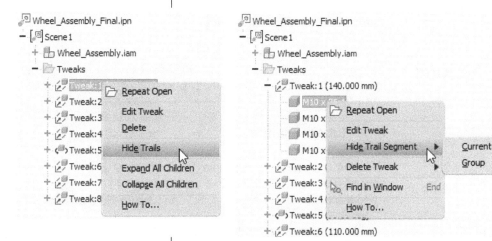

Figure 2–12

- Repeat the process using the Model Browser and use **Show Trail Segment** to return the display of trail lines to the model.

Deleting Tweaks

Similar to controlling the visibility of the trail lines in a tweak, you have multiple methods that can be used to delete individual and groups of tweaks from a presentation.

- In the graphic window, right-click a trail line and select **Delete Tweak**. Using this method, you can delete the tweak for the selected trail line using the **Current** option or delete all tweaks in the group using the **Group** option.

- In the Model Browser, expand the *Tweaks* folder, right-click a tweak and select **Delete**. All tweaks in the group are deleted.

- In the Model Browser, expand the *Tweaks* folder and **Tweak** node, right-click a component and select **Delete Tweak**.

- In the timeline, right-click on the tweak symbol and select **Delete**. You can specify it the Tweak for the current component (**Current**) or all components in the group are to be deleted (**Group**).

> **Hint: Aligning Start/End Time**
>
> To quickly align two Tweaks to either start or end at the same time, select them using <Ctrl>, right-click, and select **Align Start Time** or **Align End Time**.

Actions

Actions can be added to the timeline of a storyboard to control the appearance of components throughout an animation, or a camera position.

Model Appearance

To begin, place the timeliner playhead at the location that the action will be assigned. Actions that customize the model's appearance (visibility and opacity) can be added as follows:

*If a component was set as **Transparent** in the source assembly, that setting is visible if used in a presentation.*

- To change component opacity, select the component, and in the Component panel, click ⊞ (Opacity). Use the Opacity mini-toolbar (shown in Figure 2–13) to specify the opacity value. You can use the slider or enter a value in the entry field. Click ✓ to complete the modification. Opacity actions are identified with the ▢ symbol in the timeline and are initially set as instant actions.

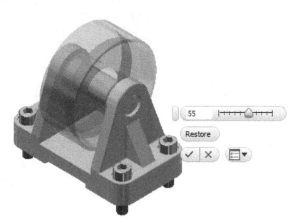

Figure 2–13

*Multiple Opacity settings can be modified at once by preselecting them prior to selecting **Edit Opacity**.*

*The **Edit Time** option for a Visibility action only enables you to change the time to an exact value. You cannot set a Visibility action for a duration. If the visibility is to be returned, move the playhead to the time, and toggle on the component's visibility.*

- To clear the visibility of a component, select the component in the graphic window or Model Browser, right-click and select **Visibility**. This removes the component from display in the animation at the point where the playhead was located.

  Visibility actions are identified with the  symbol in the timeline and can only be instantaneous.

- To modify a Visibility or Opacity action, move the playhead to its location on the timeline, select the component, and use the **Opacity** and **Visibility** options a second time.

- By default, an Opacity action is set to be instantaneous; however, it can be modified to run over a specified duration.

  To edit the action, right-click the ▥ symbol in the timeline and select **Edit Time**. In the drop-down list, change the action type to **Duration**, as shown in Figure 2–14.

Figure 2–14

- Select and drag a Visibility or Opacity action along the timeline to relocate them.

- To delete a Visibility or Opacity action, select it in the timeline, right-click, and select **Delete**.

Camera Position

An action that changes the camera position can be set to run over a specified duration. To begin, place the timeliner playhead at the location that the action will be assigned.

How To: Customize the Model's Camera Position

1. To change position of the camera, use the ViewCube or other navigation tools to change the model orientation (camera).

2. In the Camera panel, click ![icon] (Capture Camera).

The Camera Position action may look compressed at the top of the timeline if the timeline is not large enough and is showing the scroll bar.

   - The action is added to the top of the timeline at the point where the playhead was positioned, as shown in Figure 2–15. It is created to run for 3 seconds.

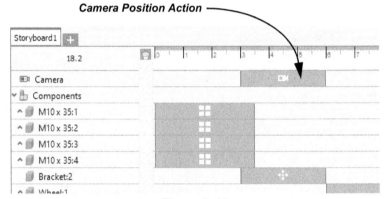

Figure 2–15

   - By default, the action is added as a Duration action. To make a change to the default duration (2.5 seconds) or change it to an Instant action, double-click the camera action on the timeline. Using the mini-toolbar (shown in Figure 2–16), you can change the type of action and its *Start*, *End,* or *Duration* times.

*Alternatively, you can right-click on a Camera Position action in the timeline and select **Edit Time** to open the mini-toolbar.*

Figure 2–16

   - Select and drag a Camera Position action to move it along the timeline.

   - To delete a Camera Position action, select it in the timeline, right-click, and select **Delete**.

Hint: Scratch Zone

The area on the timeline that displays prior to the start of the timeline is called the *Scratch Zone*. It is identified with the 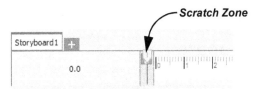 symbol, as shown in Figure 2–17. The *Scratch Zone* enables you to set the initial view settings, visibility, opacity, and camera position for the assembly. When the settings are made in the *Scratch Zone*, they are not included in the animation. It simply defines how the assembly displays at time 0 on the timeline.

Figure 2–17

- To set the options, position the playhead of the timeliner in this area, and use the **Visibility**, **Opacity**, and **Capture Camera** options, as required.

- Modifications cannot be made to the actions in the *Scratch Zone*. Use the **Visibility**, **Opacity**, and **Capture Camera** options a second time to reset them.

Hint: Deleting all Actions for a Component

Individual Tweaks and Actions can be deleted directly on the timeline. To delete all actions associated with a component, right-click on the component name in the Storyboard panel and select **Delete Actions**.

- If the current storyboard was created using **Start from end of Previous**, the **Delete Actions** option will delete all current and inherited actions from the previous storyboard.

Playing a Storyboard

Once you have created an animation and have added actions, you can use the Timeline Controls to playback the entire storyboard. The Timeline Controls are located at the top of the Storyboard panel. The options in this panel are consistent with standard playback controls (rewind to beginning, play, pause, play in reverse, and fast forward to end).

Hint: Tweak and Action Selection

To quickly select all or multiple timeline entries for editing before or after a specific entry, right-click on the entry and select **Select>All Before** or **Select>All After**. When working with groups, right-click on one entry and select **Select>Group** to select all entries in the group.

2.3 Snapshot Views

Snapshot views store a combination of component display settings and positions in one view to communicate specific information in the model. The Snapshot view can be used to create image files for presentations or views in an Inventor drawing file. To create an exploded assembly view in a drawing you must create an exploded Snapshot view and reference it in a drawing.

The component display settings that can be assigned in a Snapshot view are similar to those used to create animations. They include:

- Component positions using tweaks
- Component visibility settings
- Component opacity settings
- Camera positions defined by the model's orientation
- View settings using the *View* tab.

A Snapshot view can be created using a previously created storyboard or they can be created independently.

Creating Snapshots from a Storyboard

How To: Create a Snapshot View from a Storyboard

1. Activate the scene to which the Snapshot view will be added.
   - To activate it, double click the scene name in the Model Browser.
2. In the Timeline, position the playhead at the point at which the Snapshot view is required.
3. In the Workshop panel, click ⌐◻⌐ (New Snapshot View).

A new view is added in the Snapshot Views browser. The component display settings that exist in the storyboard at the location of the playhead are used in the Snapshot view.

*To rename a Snapshot view, right-click on its thumbnail image and select **Rename**. Enter a new descriptive name for the image and press <Enter>.*

- The ⬕ marker displays on the Snapshot view's thumbnail image, indicating that it is associated with the storyboard animation, as shown in Figure 2–18.

- The ⬕ marker also displays on the Timeline, indicating that a Snapshot view was created, as shown in Figure 2–18. The symbol can be dragged to change the snapshot location on the timeline, if required.

- If the Snapshot view marker is moved on the timeline or changes are made to any of the actions at that time, the ⊕ symbol displays on the view in the Snapshot Views browser, indicating that it is out of date. Select the symbol to update it.

Snapshot in the Snapshot Browser

View 1

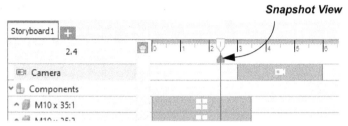

Snapshot View

Figure 2–18

Hint: Snapshot Views at the Beginning of an Animation

Snapshot views that are created when the playhead is at the beginning of the animation timeline (0 seconds) will not create a dependent Snapshot view.

Creating Independent Snapshots

How To: Create an Independent Snapshot View

1. Activate the scene to which the Snapshot view will be added.
   - To activate it, double click the scene name in the Model Browser.
2. Position the Storyboard playhead in the *Scratch Zone*, as shown in Figure 2–19.
   - If an animation or actions exist in the Storyboard, position the playhead in the *Scratch Zone*.
   - If no animation or actions exist, independent Snapshot views will be created regardless of being in the *Scratch Zone*.

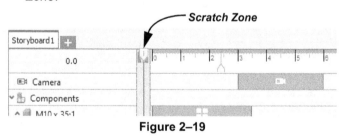

Scratch Zone

Figure 2–19

*To rename a Snapshot view, right-click on its thumbnail image and select **Rename**. Enter a new descriptive name for the image and press <Enter>.*

3. In the Workshop panel, click ⬚ (New Snapshot View). The view is added to the Snapshot Views browser. The ⬘ marker does not display on the view's thumbnail image as it does for dependent views.

Editing a Snapshot View

Snapshot views that are dependent on the Storyboard show the assembly at a specific time on the timeline. In the case of independent views, they will likely need to be customized once the view is created.

How To: Edit an Independent Snapshot View

1. Activate the scene to which the Snapshot view exists.
2. In the Snapshot Views browser, right-click the view that is to be edited and select **Edit**. Alternatively, double-click the view to edit it. The *Edit View* tab becomes the active tab (shown in Figure 2–20) and the Storyboard panel is removed from the display.

Figure 2–20

As you edit an existing view, you can click  *(New Snapshot View) in the Workshop to create an additional view.*

3. Set the component's view display using any of the following tools:

   - Use the ViewCube and Navigation bar to set the model orientation. Click (Update Camera) to update the view.
   - Select components, right-click, and clear the **Visibility** option for components that are not required in the view.
   - Select component(s) and on the Component panel, click

     (Opacity) to assign an Opacity value to component(s) in the view.
   - In the *View* tab, assign view settings from the *View* tab to customize the view.

   - Use the (Tweak Components) command to move or rotate components in the Snapshot view. Use the mini-toolbar in the same way as is done for an animation to move and rotate components in the view.

4. Click (Finish Edit View) to complete the edit.

Hint: Making a Dependent Snapshot View Independent

The ⬠ marker on a Snapshot view's thumbnail image indicates that it is associated (linked) with the storyboard animation. If you edit this type of view, you will be prompted that you cannot make changes to a view that is linked to the timeline (as shown in Figure 2–21). To permanently break the link, click **Break Link**.

Figure 2–21

The ⬠ marker is removed from the Snapshot view's thumbnail image. Only the addition of a tweak or the change of Opacity and Visibility for a component require you to break the link. Changes to the camera position/orientation are permitted without breaking the link.

Creating a Drawing View from a Snapshot View

Creating drawings will be discussed in more detail later in the guide.

Any of the Snapshot views listed in the Snapshot Views browser can be used to create a drawing view.

• The Snapshot view's name can be selected in the *Presentation* area of the Drawing View dialog box when an .IPN file is selected as the drawing model, as shown in Figure 2–22.

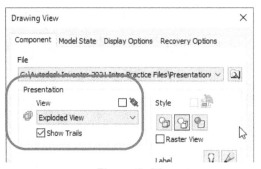

Figure 2–22

• A drawing view can also be created directly from the Presentation file using the following:

  • In the Snapshot Views browser, right-click on the thumbnail image and select **Create Drawing View**. The drawing view will be created using this Snapshot view.

- While editing a Snapshot view, in the *Edit View* tab> Drawing panel, click ⬚ (Create Drawing View). The drawing view will be created using this Snapshot view.

- In the *Presentation* tab>Drawing panel, click ⬚ (Create Drawing View). The drawing view will be created and defaults to using the first Snapshot view. You can select an alternate, if required.

Once the command is selected, you will be prompted to select a drawing template for the new drawing and then you will be immediately placed in the drawing. The Drawing View dialog box opens and you can begin to place the Base view and any additional Projected views, as shown in Figure 2–23.

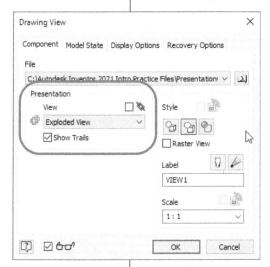

Figure 2–23

The *Presentation* area of the dialog box displays the name of the Snapshot view being used. Consider the following:

- Select an alternate Snapshot view in the drop-down list.

- Show or clear the trails in the view using **Show Trails**. Trails can only be controlled if they exist in the Snapshot view.

- Select ⬚ to set the new view as associative. This ensures that if a change is made to the Snapshot view in the Presentation file, it will update the drawing view.

2.4 Publishing a Presentation File

Both Snapshot views and Storyboards can be published to various formats. Snapshot views can be published as raster images and Storyboards can be published as animations.

How To: Publish Snapshot Views

1. Activate the scene in which the Snapshot will be published.
2. Select the view(s) to publish in the Snapshot Views browser.
   - To publish multiple Snapshot views, press and hold <Ctrl> during selection.

A Snapshot view can be published while it is being edited by selecting ▦ (Raster) in the Edit View tab.

3. Open the Publish to Raster Images dialog box, as shown in Figure 2–24 to publish the snapshots.
   - In the *Presentation* tab>Publish panel, click ▦ (Raster).
   - Right-click a view in the Snapshot Views browser and select **Publish to Raster**.

Figure 2–24

4. In the the *Publish Scope* area, define the scope of publishing.
   - Click **All Views** to publish all Snapshot views available in active scene.

- Use **Selected Views** to publish the views that were previously selected.

5. In the *Image Resolution* area, define the image size.

   - Use **Current Document Window Size** in the drop-down list to publish the view as it is currently displayed.
   - Select a predefined image size in the drop-down list.
   - Select **Custom** in the drop-down list and enter a custom *Width*, *Height*, and *Resolution* value by pixel or unit size.
   - Enter a *Resolution* value.

6. In the *Output* area, specify a folder to save the file. The Snapshot view name will be used as the published filename.
7. In the File Format drop-down list, select a publishing format.
8. Enable **Transparent Background**, if required.
9. Click **OK** to publish the image.

The supported image file formats include BMP, GIF, JPEG, PNG, or TIFF.

How To: Publish a Storyboard

1. Activate the scene in which the Storyboard will be published.
2. In the Storyboard panel, select the *Storyboard* tab that is to be published.
3. Open the Publish to Video dialog box, as shown in Figure 2–25 to publish the snapshots.

*The **Video** option is only available if an animation exists in the Storyboard panel.*

- In the *Presentation* tab>Publish panel, click  (Video).
- Right-click a *Storyboard* tab and select **Publish**.

Figure 2–25

4. In the *Publish Scope* area, define the scope of publishing.
   - Use **All Storyboard** to publish all storyboards available in active scene.
   - Use **Current Storyboard** to publish the active storyboard.
   - Use **Current Storyboard Range** to publish a time range in the active storyboard. Enter values in the *From* and *To* fields.
   - Click **Reverse** to publish the video in a reverse order (end to start).
5. In the *Video Resolution* area, define the video size.
   - Use **Current Document Window Size** in the drop-down list to publish the video as it is currently displayed.
   - Select a predefined video size in the drop-down list.
   - Select **Custom** in the drop-down list and enter a custom *Width*, *Height*, and *Resolution* value by pixel or unit size.
6. In *Output* area, specify a name for the video and a folder to save the file.
7. In the File Format drop-down list, select a publishing format.
8. Click **OK** to publish the video.
9. For AVI formatted videos, select a video compressor and set compression quality, if available. Click **OK**.

The supported video file formats include WMV and AVI. A WMV video player must be installed on your computer to publish to WMV format.

Practice 2a

Create an Animation

Practice Objectives

- Create a new presentation file using a standard template.
- Create an animation that explodes the components of an assembly using translational and rotational movements.
- Control the visual display and orientation of components in an animation.
- Play an animation and then publish it.

In this practice, you will create a presentation file using a wheel assembly. The assembly file that will be used is shown in Figure 2–26. Using the tools in the Presentation file, you will create an animation that explodes the components of the assembly to show how it is assembled.

A video called video2.wmv has been provided in the Presentation folder of the practice files folder for you to review the animation that will be created in this practice.

Figure 2–26

Task 1 - Create a presentation file.

Alternatively, use the Quick Access toolbar, File menu, or the My Home tab to create a new file.

1. In the *Get Started* tab>Launch panel, click ☐ (New).

2. Select the *Metric* folder, select **Standard(mm).ipn** in the Create New File dialog box to create a new presentation file, and click **Create**.

   - You might need to scroll down in the list to locate this template.

*If a specific representation of the file is to be used, click **Options** and select the required Design View, Level of Detail, or Positional Representation to use.*

3. In the Insert dialog box, navigate to the *Presentation* folder and select **Wheel_Assembly.iam**. Click **Open**.

    - The presentation environment displays and the *Presentation* tab is the active tab.
    - By default, there is a single scene created using the wheel assembly and **Storyboard1** is active. No snapshots are initially created.

Task 2 - Define the initial model display for the animation.

1. The playhead ( ) starts at time 0 seconds. Drag the playhead to the left into the (*Scratch Zone*) area of the panel, as shown in Figure 2–27.

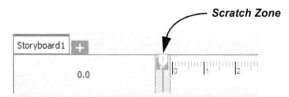

Figure 2–27

The Scratch Zone is where you can set the initial visibility, opacity, and camera position for the model.

2. Rotate the model into a custom orientation using the ViewCube. Select the corner shown in Figure 2–28. This positions the model for the start of the animation.

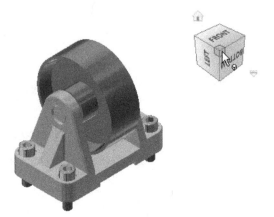

Figure 2–28

3. In the Camera panel, click (Capture Camera). This stores the orientation for the start position of the animation.

Task 3 - Create an exploded animation of the assembly.

1. Expand the **Scene1** node in the Model Browser and the **Wheel_Assembly.iam** node. All of the assembly component's names display. This provides a convenient way to select components.

2. To move components, in the *Presentation* tab>Component panel, click ⊞ (Tweak Components). The Tweak Component mini-toolbar opens as shown in Figure 2–29.

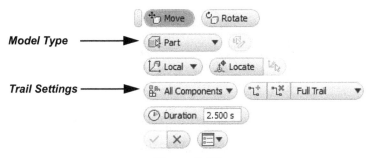

Figure 2–29

3. Ensure that **Part** is selected in the Model Type drop-down list.

4. Press and hold <Ctrl> and select the four **M10 x 35** components in the Model Browser. All the components should be highlighted in the model and the tweak triad should be displayed.

5. Ensure that **Move** is selected in the top row of the mini-toolbar to move components in either the X, Y, or Z directions.

6. Expand the Trail Settings drop-down list in the mini-toolbar. The options in this field enables you to customize if trails are created. In this practice, they will be created and you will later learn how to quickly toggle them on and off. Ensure that **All Components** is selected.

7. The triad orientation displays the local coordinate system for the part. Expand the **Local** option and select **World** to change the orientation of the triad to be consistent with the assembly coordinate system.

*Alternatively, you can use the **Select Other** tool in the graphics window to select any hidden components to avoid rotating the model and changing its orientation in the animation.*

8. Select the arrow that points in the Z direction relative to the assembly's origin, as shown in Figure 2–30.

    • If the model origin is not displayed, consider toggling it on in the Application Options>*Display* tab>**Show Origin 3D indicator**.

Depending on the order in which the components are selected, the triad may display in a different location or orientation.

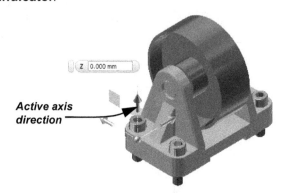

Figure 2–30

9. The active Z axis direction displays in gold. Drag the arrowhead upwards to move the four components. Enter **75** (or **-75**) in the *Z* entry field to move the components a specific distance.

10. Click ✔ to complete the Tweak and close the mini-toolbar.

Tweak actions are set at 2.5 seconds by default. This can be modified in the Tweak mini-toolbar prior to closing it or it can be modified after it is created.

11. Note that the four components are listed in the Storyboard panel and the tweak actions are scheduled to last 2.5 seconds, as shown in Figure 2–31.

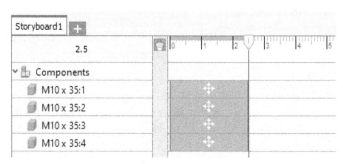

Figure 2–31

12. Hover the cursor over the Tweak action (⊞) for the first component in the list, right-click, and select **Edit Time**.

13. In the mini-toolbar, set the *Duration* value to **3.00**. Click .

14. The first component is now set to get into its exploded position slower than the others. Click ◁ in the playback controls to rewind the timeline to the beginning and click ▷. Note the differences in the timing.

15. Hover the cursor over the Tweak action () for the second component in the list and double-click to edit it. This is an alternative method to edit the timing.

16. Set the *Duration* value to **3.00**. Click ✓.

17. Hold <Ctrl> and select the third and fourth component's Tweak actions (⊕), hover the cursor over the right-hand edge of the action bar. Drag to the right to manually extend its duration. Ensure that it snaps to 3 seconds. The Storyboard panel should display as shown in Figure 2–32.

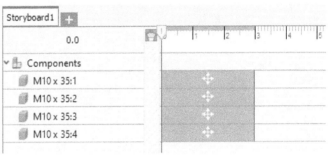

Figure 2–32

18. The fasteners have not been moved high enough. Right-click on any of the actions (⊕) and select **Edit Tweak**.

19. In the *Distance* field, enter **140mm** as the new value. Click ✓. Because they are a group, they all are edited together.

Task 4 - Add additional tweaks to components.

---

1. Click ◁ to move the playhead to the end of the current actions. This ensures that the next tweak is added immediately at the end of the last tweak.

2. In the Component panel, click 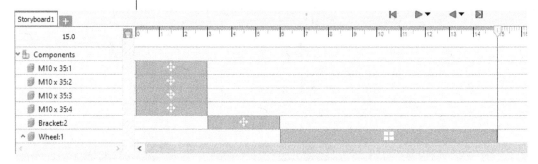 (Tweak Components). Using the following table, move and rotate the Bracket and Wheel components. The Storyboard timeline and component display should display as shown in Figure 2–33 after the two components are tweaked. Use the World coordinate system when tweaking. You might need to enter positive or negative tweak values to translate and rotate as shown.

Ensure that the playhead is at the correct position on the timeline when defining each tweak.

Component	Tweaks
Bracket:2	• Translate 175mm along the X-axis. • Define the tweak as 3.00 seconds.
Wheel	• Translate 110 mm along the X-axis. • Translate 120 mm along the Z axis. • Rotate 90 degrees in the XZ plane. • Modify each tweak to 3.00 seconds, if not already set.

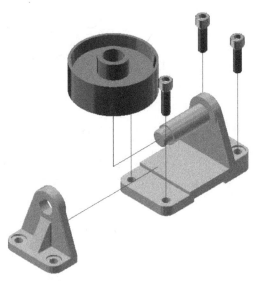

Figure 2–33

3. Play the animation from the beginning and note how the wheel is unassembled with three actions that occur consecutively. After playing, note that the model displays reassembled. This is only because the playhead returns to where it starts on the timeline. The animation will end fully disassembled at 15 seconds once published.

4. The three actions for the Wheel are grouped. In the Storyboard, expand the **Wheel** component in the component list to show the individual actions. To manipulate them, it must be expanded.

5. Manipulate the duration of the rotation action ( ) and relocate it on the timeline such that it occurs while the component is moving in the Z direction, similar to that shown in Figure 2–34.

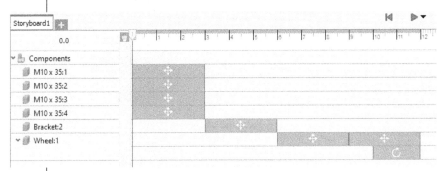

Figure 2–34

6. Use the following table to apply tweaks to the remaining components. The components should display as shown in Figure 2–35 after the remaining three components are tweaked. Use the World coordinate system when tweaking the components. You might need to enter positive or negative tweak values to translate and rotate as shown.

Ensure that the playhead is at the correct position on the timeline when defining each tweak.

Component	Tweaks
Axle	• Translate 110mm along the X-axis. • Define the tweak as 3.00 seconds.
Bracket:1	• Translate 110mm along the X-axis. • Define the tweak as 2.50 seconds.
Plate	• Translate 80 mm along the Z axis. • Define the tweak as 2.50 seconds.

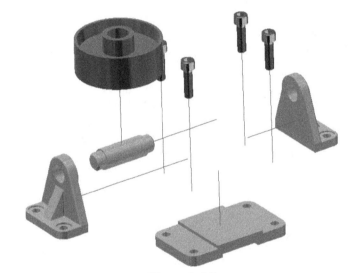

Figure 2–35

7. Manipulate the timeline such that the last two components assemble at the same time and run for 2.00 seconds.

8. Play the animation and verify that it functions as expected.
   • A video called **video1.wmv** has been provided in the practice files folder for you to compare with.

9. Save the presentation file using its default name into the *Presentation* folder.

Task 5 - Incorporate visual changes in the animation.

1. In the Model Browser, right-click on the *Tweaks* folder and select **Hide All Trails**, as shown in Figure 2–36. If **Hide All Trails** is not available, move your playhead past the start of the timeline and try again.

If you were to expand the Tweaks folder, it lists all tweaks that were created and you can individually edit them or hide their trail lines.

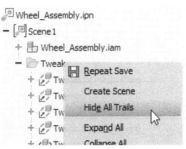

Figure 2–36

2. Return the playhead to the beginning of the timeline and play the animation. Note that the trail lines are all removed from the display.

3. Once the fasteners are exploded, they can fade from the display. Place the playhead at **3s** and select all four fasteners.

4. In the Component panel, click (Opacity). When prompted that the scene is associated with a design view and that you must break or override the associativity, click **Break**. This makes the scene independent of the Master Design View that was imported into the scene.

5. On the mini-toolbar, drag the *Opacity* slider to **0**. Click ✓.

6. Note how the new component opacity action is grouped with the other actions for these components. Expand the first component, as shown in Figure 2–37.

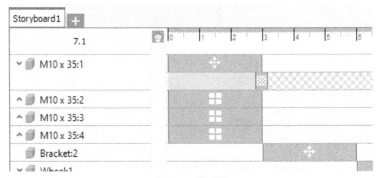

Figure 2–37

7. Right-click on the action for the first fastener and select **Edit Time**. By default, the action is created as an Instant action.

8. Select **Duration** in the drop-down list in the mini-toolbar.

9. Set the *Start* value to **2.50** and the *End* value to **3.50**. Click ✓.

10. Play the animation and note the difference between the first fastener's visibility changes and the other fasteners.

11. Modify the other three fasteners such that they also fade out over a duration of 2.50 to 3.50 seconds.

12. Compress the **M10 x 35** component nodes in the Storyboard panel once your edits are complete.

Task 6 - Spin the model at the end of the animation.
---

1. Click 🏳 to move the playhead to the end of the animation.

2. Reorient the model to the orientation shown on the ViewCube in Figure 2–38 and zoom in on the model.

Figure 2–38

As an alternative to using opacity, you could have also cleared the visibility of the components at a specific time. The Visibility action is only instantaneous.

3. In the Camera panel, click (Capture Camera). A camera action is added to the top of the timeline.

4. Modify the length of the camera action by right-clicking on the symbol and selecting **Edit Time**.

5. Modify the duration to start at 16 seconds and last until 19 seconds. Alternatively, you can drag the action and extend its action on the timeline.

6. Move the playhead to the beginning of the animation. The entire timeline should display similar to that shown in Figure 2–39.

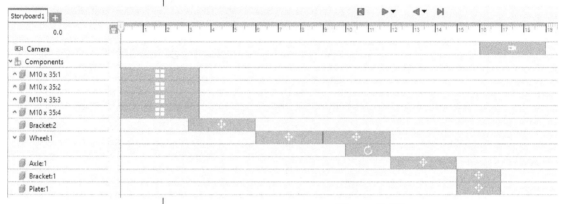

Figure 2–39

7. Play the animation to see how this new Camera action affects the animation.
   - A video called **video2.wmv** has been provided in the practice files folder for you to compare with.

Task 7 - Modify the View settings in the model.

---

1. Return the playhead into the *Scratch Zone* once again.

2. On the ribbon, select the *View* tab. Use the tools in the Appearance panel to set the following:

   - In the Shadows drop-down list, enable **Ambient Shadows**.
   - In the Visual Style drop-down list, select **Technical Illustration** or an alternate style. Note that threads do not display in a technical illustration.

3. Play the animation.

The settings that are defined in the View tab are temporary and are not saved with the Presentation file.

Task 8 - Publish the Storyboard.

1. In the *Presentation* tab>Publish panel, click (Video). Alternatively, right-click on the *Storyboard1* tab and select **Publish to Video**.

2. In the Publish to Video dialog box, ensure that **Current Storyboard** is selected in the *Publish Scope* area.

3. In the *Video Resolution* area, maintain the **Current Document Window Size** option to publish the video as it is currently displayed.

4. In the *Output* area, set the video name to **my_wheel_assembly** and save it to the *Presentation* folder in the practice files folder.

5. In the File Format drop-down list, select **WMV File (*.wmv)**.

6. Click **OK** to publish the video.

7. Navigate to the *Presentation* folder in the practice files and play the video once it has published.

8. Save the presentation file and close the window.

Practice 2b | Create Snapshots

Practice Objectives

- Create snapshots that are dependent on a storyboard animation.
- Create snapshots that are independent from a storyboard animation.
- Edit snapshots to manipulate component position and component display.
- Update snapshots that are dependent on a storyboard animation.

In this practice, you will create Snapshot views that are both dependent on an animation as well as independent of it. You will also learn how to edit both types of Snapshot views using the tools available in the Presentation environment. The independent exploded Snapshot view is shown in Figure 2–40.

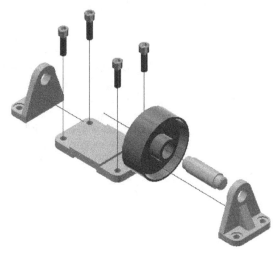

Figure 2–40

Task 1 - Create Snapshot Views that are dependent on a Storyboard animation.

In this task, you will create multiple Snapshot views all based on the storyboard animation that already exists in the presentation file.

1. Continue working with the Presentation file from the previous practice or open **Wheel_Assembly_Final.ipn** from the *Presentation* folder.

2. Note that there is currently one scene in the file (**Scene1**) and that this scene does not currently have any Snapshot views in the Snapshot Views browser.

3. In the timeline, move the playhead to the beginning of the animation (0 seconds). You can select ◄ or simply drag the playhead to the beginning of the animation.

4. In the Workshop panel, click ⊡ (New Snapshot View).

5. **View1** is added to the Snapshot Views browser. Right-click on the **View1** thumbnail image and select **Rename**. Set the new name to **Fully Assembled**.

6. Move the playhead to approximately 2.5 seconds. This should show the fasteners exploded, but not yet set to an Opacity value of 0.

7. In the Workshop panel, click ⊡ (New Snapshot View).

8. **View2** is added to the Snapshot Views browser. The ⌂ marker displays on the Snapshot view's thumbnail image, indicating that it is associated with the storyboard animation. Snapshot views created at 0 seconds are not associative to the storyboard.

9. Select the view label for the **View2** thumbnail image. Set the new name to **Step1**. This is an alternative to using the **Rename** command.

Snapshot views can also be created by right-clicking on the playhead in the timeline.

10. Using the steps previously described, create the following snapshots. The Snapshots Views browser should display similar to that shown Figure 2–41.

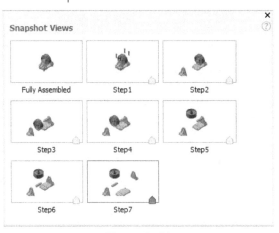

Figure 2–41

Time (seconds)	Snapshot View Name
6	Step2
9	Step3
10	Step4
12	Step5
15	Step6
16	Step7

11. Refer to the Snapshot Views browser and the Storyboard timeline and note the following:

- The 🔵 marker that displays on the last view (**Step7**) is blue and the outline of the view is also blue, indicating that the view is active.

- The ⬜ markers displays along the timeline, showing the locations where the snapshots were taken.

Task 2 - Modify a dependent snapshot view.

Between 15s and 16s, both the second **Bracket** and the **Plate** are moved apart. For static images, only the **Bracket** needs to be moved. The animation is to stay as it is; however, you will edit the Step 7 view to make the change.

1. Right-click on the **Step7** thumbnail image and select **Edit**. The *Edit View* tab is activated, as shown in Figure 2–42

Figure 2–42

2. Select the **Plate** component in the graphics window. Right-click and select **Delete Tweak>Last**.

3. When prompted that you cannot make changes to a view that is linked to the timeline, click **Break Link** to permanently break the link. The **Plate** component returns to its original position. No other changes are required in this view.

4. In the Exit panel, click ✅ (Finish Edit View).

5. Note that the **Step7** view no longer has the 🔵 marker. This indicates that it is now an independent view.

Task 3 - Modify actions on the timeline.

1. In the timeline, expand the four **M10 x 35** components.

2. Right-click on the ▢ symbol for the first component, right-click and select **Delete**, as shown in Figure 2–43. The first fastener is returned to the model display.

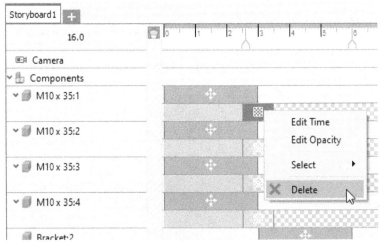

Figure 2–43

3. Delete the three other Opacity actions for the other fasteners. To delete the three fasteners at once, press and hold <Ctrl> to select them prior to selecting **Delete**. Five of the Snapshot views that are dependent on the timeline now show the ⟳ symbol on their thumbnail image, as shown in Figure 2–44.

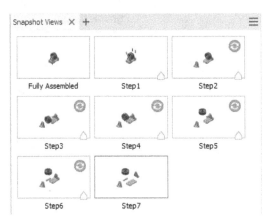

Figure 2–44

4. Select the ⊕ symbol on each thumbnail image to update them to reflect the change in the animation.

Task 4 - Modify the orientation of a model in a Snapshot view.

1. Double-click on the **Step6** thumbnail image in the Snapshot Views browser to edit it.

2. Using the ViewCube, rotate the model into an alternate position so that you can see all of the fasteners. In the Camera panel, click ⬚ (Update Camera). Note that the view changes in the thumbnail image and you were not prompted that the change would require you to break the link to the animation. Camera position changes do not affect the associativity with the animation.

3. In the Exit panel, click ✓ (Finish Edit View).

Task 5 - Create an independent view.

In this task, you will create a new Snapshot view that is independent of the timeline. You will then explode the assembly to create an alternate explode view that can be used in a drawing.

1. In the timeline, move the playhead to the beginning of the animation (0 seconds).

2. Create a new Snapshot view and rename it to **Exploded View**.

3. Edit the new Exploded View.

For more detail on tweaking components, refer to Practice 20a.

4. Rotate the model and use the  (Tweak Components) command to explode the components similar to that shown in Figure 2–45.

   - When creating the exploded view, create it with visible trail lines.

Figure 2–45

5. In the Camera panel, click (Update Camera).

6. Finish the edit to return to the *Presentation* tab.

7. Save the presentation file and close the window.

> **Hint: Creating a drawing view from a Snapshot view.**
>
> A Snapshot view can be created directly from a presentation file using the **Create Drawing View** option. Drawing views are discussed further in a later chapter.

Chapter Review Questions

1. Which of the following file formats is used to create an exploded assembly model in a Drawing view?

    a. .IAM

    b. .IPT

    c. .IPN

    d. .DWG

2. What is the purpose of a Presentation file? (Select all that apply.)

    a. To simplify the display of an assembly.

    b. To create an Exploded View of an assembly.

    c. To update an assembly more quickly.

    d. To create an animation of an assembly.

    e. To help document and visualize the assembly.

3. Which of the following statements are true regarding a Presentation file? (Select all that apply.)

    a. Once the Presentation template is selected for use, you are immediately prompted to open the model that will be used in **Scene1** of the presentation.

    b. A Snapshot view that is oriented in the model's Home view is automatically added to a new Presentation file.

    c. Multiple storyboards can be created in a presentation file to document an assembly.

    d. Storyboard animations can be used in a drawing view.

4. It is not possible to edit a Snapshot view that was created dependent on a specific time in an animation.

    a. True

    b. False

5. Which command enables you to save a specific view orientation at a set time in an animation?

    a. **New Storyboard**

    b. **New Snapshot View**

    c. **Tweak Components**

    d. **Capture Camera**

6. What is the purpose of adding a trail?

    a. To define a path for an animation.

    b. To move the position of a component.

    c. To change the color of a component.

    d. To help define the relationships between the components in terms of how they are assembled.

7. To create an animated assembly of a model's assembly process, you must create an animation that uses the _____ command.

    a. **New Storyboard**

    b. **Tweak Components**

    c. **Opacity**

    d. **Capture Camera**

8. Which of the following are valid methods to change the duration of an action in a storyboard animation? (Select all that apply.)

    a. Enter a *Duration* value in the mini-toolbar during Tweak creation.

    b. Use the **Edit Tweak** command and enter a new *Duration* value.

    c. Use the **Edit Time** command and enter a new *Duration* value.

    d. Drag the action's duration directly in the timeline.

9. **Move** and **Rotate** tweaks can be assigned to the same component at one time.

    a. True

    b. False

10. Which type of view setting can only be instantaneous when assigned to an animation?

    a. Opacity

    b. Visibility

Command Summary

Button	Command	Location
	Capture Camera	• **Ribbon:** *Presentation* tab>Camera panel • **Ribbon:** *Edit View* tab>Camera panel • **Context Menu**
	Create Drawing View	• **Ribbon:** *Presentation* tab>Drawing panel • **Ribbon:** *Edit View* tab>Drawing panel • **Snapshot Views browser:** right-click on a view • **Context Menu**
N/A	Delete (Tweak)	• **Timeline:** *right-click a tweak symbol* • **Model browser:** right-click on a Tweak • Graphics Window: right-click a component
N/A	Edit Time	• **Timeline:** *right-click a tweak symbol* • **Model browser:** right-click on a Tweak • Graphics Window: right-click a component
N/A	Edit Tweak	• **Timeline:** *right-click a tweak symbol* • **Model browser:** right-click on a Tweak
N/A	Hide Trails /Hide Trail Segments	• **Model browser:** right-click on a Tweak • Graphics Window: right-click a component
	New Snapshot View	• **Ribbon:** *Presentation* tab>Workshop panel • **Ribbon:** *Edit View* tab>Workshop panel • **Context Menu** • Storyboard Panel (right-click on the playhead ⬇)
	New Storyboard	• **Ribbon:** *Presentation* tab>Workshop panel • **Context Menu** • Storyboard Panel (click [+])
	Opacity	• **Ribbon:** *Presentation* tab>Component panel with a component selected • **Ribbon:** *Edit View* tab>Component panel with a component selected • **Context Menu** with a component selected
	Raster	• **Ribbon:** *Presentation* tab>Publish panel • **Ribbon:** *Edit View* tab>Publish panel • **Context Menu**
	Tweak Components	• **Ribbon:** *Presentation* tab>Component panel • **Ribbon:** *Edit View* tab>Component panel • **Context Menu**

	Video	• **Ribbon:** *Presentation* tab>Publish panel
		• **Ribbon:** *Edit View* tab>Publish panel
		• **Context Menu**
		• **Storyboard Panel** (right-click on the tab)
N/A	Visibility	• **Context Menu** with a component selected
		• **Model browser** with a component selected

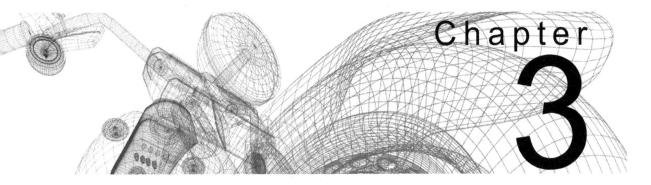

Inventor Studio

Inventor Studio enables you to create realistic renderings or animations of models. To render images, you can set the surface styles, lighting styles, appearance, resolution, and camera views. To animate models, a number of rendered images are compiled to create an AVI file.

Learning Objectives in This Chapter

- Render a realistic image of a model that has had appearance, lighting, and camera customizations assigned.
- Create a realistic animation of a model to display its range of motion, assembly process, or other movement by applying parameters, constraints, and actions.
- Create a composite video by combining camera shots, animations, and transitions using the Video Producer.
- Create a room assembly as a custom environment for use when rendering models.

3.1 Rendering

Renderings help visualize a model's appearance before it is manufactured. You can apply different appearances, lighting styles, cameras, and local lights to create a realistic environment for the model.

General Steps

Use the following general steps to render an image:

1. Apply appearances.
2. Define the Studio Lighting Styles.
3. Define cameras.
4. Define local lights.
5. Render the image.
6. Save the image.

Step 1 - Apply appearances.

New appearances can be applied using two techniques:

- Select a part or subassembly in the Model Browser and select an override material from the Quick Access Toolbar's Appearance Override drop-down list, as shown in Figure 3–1.

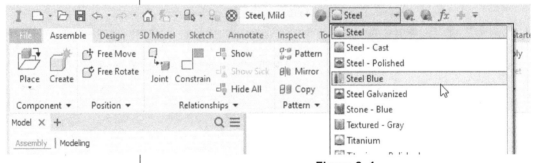

Figure 3–1

- Click ⬤ (Appearance) in the *Tools* tab>Material and Appearance panel or the Quick Access toolbar, to open the Appearance Browser, as shown in Figure 3–2. From this dialog box you can add appearances to the document and then to a component.

  - To add a appearance to the document, right-click on an appearance in the Material Library and click **Add to> Document Materials**.
  - To assign the appearance to a component, select a component, right-click on the material in the *Document Appearances* area and select **Assign to Selection**.

To clear the appearance overrides, click

⬤ (Clear) in the Tools tab>Material and Appearance panel, or in the Quick Access toolbar, and select the objects that you want to clear.

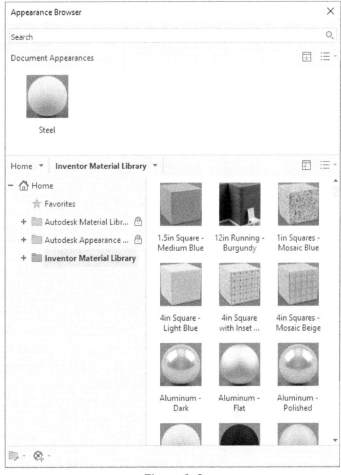

Figure 3–2

Step 2 - Define the Studio Lighting Styles.

With a model open, select the *Environments* tab and click

 (Inventor Studio). The *Render* contextual tab is activated.

In the Scene panel, click (Studio Lighting Styles). The Lighting Styles dialog box opens, as shown in Figure 3–3. All default lighting styles in Inventor Studio use Image-Based Lighting (IBL). They do not contain any local lights.

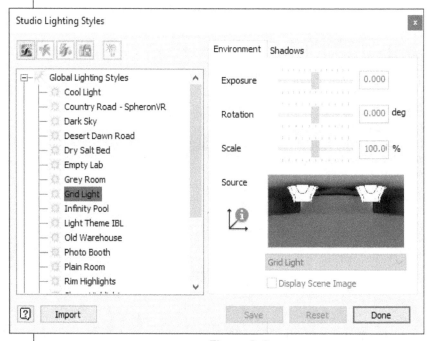

Figure 3–3

- The Studio Lighting Styles dialog box lists the available lighting styles in two categories:
  - Global Lighting Styles are styles that are provided with the software.
  - Local Lighting Styles are styles that exist in the current file.

- A style must be listed in the Local Lighting Styles list to be used or modified for use in the model.

- Use any of the following methods to add a lighting style to the Local Lighting Styles list for use in the model:
  - Right-click on a Global Lighting Style and select **Active**.
  - Right-click on a Global Lighting Style and select **Copy Lighting Style** and enter a new name.
  - Right-click on a Global Lighting Style and select **New Lighting Style**.
  - Click 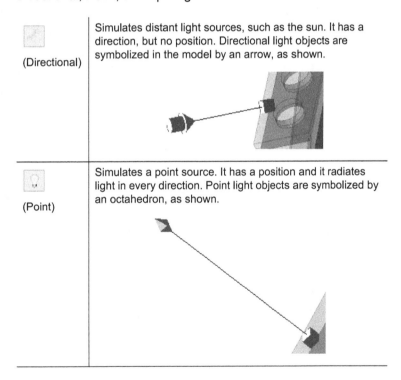 (New Lighting Style) in the dialog box.

When activating or copying a lighting style to the local list, only the IBL environment is added. When using either of the **New Lighting Style** options, you are provided with the Grid Light IBL and three lights: directional, point, and spot. Each light has application default settings. By default, the directional, point, and spot lights are toggled off. You can toggle them on by changing individual light properties.

Directional, Point, and Spot lights are described as follows:

(Directional)	Simulates distant light sources, such as the sun. It has a direction, but no position. Directional light objects are symbolized in the model by an arrow, as shown.
(Point)	Simulates a point source. It has a position and it radiates light in every direction. Point light objects are symbolized by an octahedron, as shown.

(Spot)

Simulates a spot light with a position and direction. A Spot light emits light in the shape of a cone with two degrees of intensity. The most intense area is located within the inner area of the cone and the less intense area is located within the outer area of the cone of light. Spot light objects are symbolized by a cone, as shown.

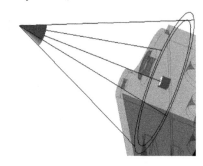

Adding Additional Lights

To create a new light in any selected lighting style, select the lighting style and click (New Light). The Light dialog box opens, as shown in Figure 3–4.

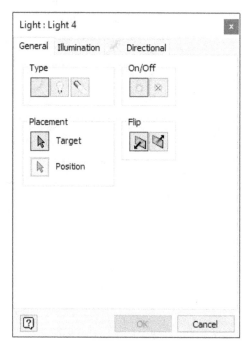

Figure 3–4

Use the following tabs to define the lighting style:

- Use the *General* tab to define the type of light as Directional ( ), Point ( ), or Spot ( ). Select an edge or face as a target reference for the light, and then select a position along the reference line. Toggle the light on and off, and flip the direction of the light.

- Use the *Illumination* tab to adjust the intensity and color.

- Use the *Directional*, *Point*, or *Spot* tab to set options specific to the type of light that is selected. The tab name changes depending on the type of light being created. The options available in this tab enable you control the position and direction of the light as well as the light's specific properties.

Setting the Environment

Once a Global lighting style has been copied to the Local Lighting style list, you can edit the options on the *Environment* tab, as follows:

- To customize its exposure, rotation, and scale, modify the values or drag the scroll bar.
- Select the **Display Scene Image** option to display the image in the graphics window.
- To change the lighting style source image, select a new one using the drop-down list. If changed, any custom lights that were added are maintained.

Shadows

Use the *Shadows* tab to define the softness setting for the lighting style.

Saving Changes

Once you are finished adding additional lights, you can click **OK** to close the Light dialog box and return to the Studio Lighting Styles. Click **Save** to save any changes made to the lighting styles. When the required lighting effect has been achieved, save any changes and click **Done**.

Step 3 - Define cameras.

Cameras enable you to save particular viewpoints of the model so that they are available when rendering.

How To: Create a Camera

1. Click ⬚ (Camera) in the Scene panel. The Camera dialog box opens as shown in Figure 3–5.

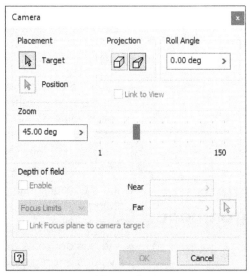

Figure 3–5

2. Select a face or edge as the Target for the camera.
3. Select a location along the reference line where the camera is going to be placed, as shown in Figure 3–6.

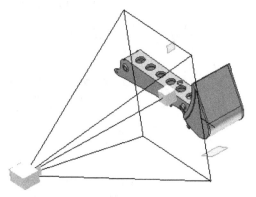

Figure 3–6

4. Define the Projection type:

- Orthographic (⬚) projects edges parallel to each other.

- Perspective (⬚) projects edges to a vanishing point, giving the perception of depth.

5. Edit the values in the *Roll Angle* field to change rotation of the camera about the reference line, as shown in Figure 3–7 (30 degrees).

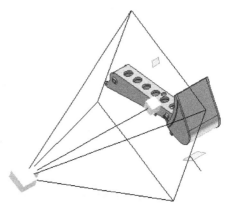

Figure 3–7

6. Adjust the zoom angle by entering an angle in the *Zoom* field, using the zoom slider, or by dragging the zoom area shown in Figure 3–8.

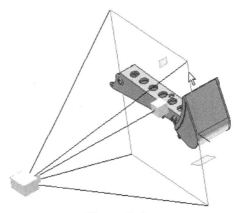

Figure 3–8

7. For Perspective projection, enable or disable the Depth of Field. These options control which objects display in focus when the image is rendered.
8. Click **OK** to save the changes. Create additional cameras as required.

Modifying a Camera

You can adjust the location and orientation of a camera by selecting it, right-clicking and selecting **Edit**.

- Use the Camera dialog box to make changes to the original settings.

- Select the camera in the graphics window to move it using the triad or the 3D Move/Rotate mini-toolbar.

- Select the target in the graphics window to move it using the triad or the 3D Move/Rotate mini-toolbar.

Step 4 - Define local lights.

To create a local light, click 🔱 (Local Lights) in the Scene panel. The Local Lights dialog box opens as shown in Figure 3–9.

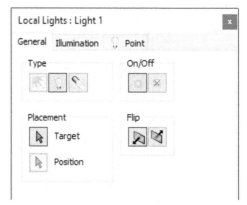

Figure 3–9

- The Local Lights dialog box contains the same options as the Light dialog box used when defining Lighting Styles, except that directional lights are not available.

- Local lights are contained in the assembly or component file and not in a Lighting Style.

- Local lights move with a component when animated.

Step 5 - Render the image.

After defining the appropriate appearances, lighting styles, cameras, and local lights, you can render the image. In the

Render panel, click 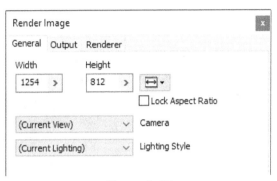 (Render Image). The Render Image dialog box opens as shown in Figure 3–10.

Render Image   x

General   Output   Renderer

Width   Height

1254   >   812   >   ⟷ ▾

                            ☐ Lock Aspect Ratio

(Current View)   ∨   Camera

(Current Lighting)   ∨   Lighting Style

Figure 3–10

Rendering Images

Use the following three tabs to define the options for rendering an image:

- Use the *General* tab to specify the width and height of the image you are rendering or use the Select Output Size list. You can also lock the aspect ratio and specify the Camera and Lighting Style.

- Use the *Output* tab to specify whether or not to save the image once it is rendered. If saved, you can enter a name and location for the file.

- Use the *Renderer* tab to control the render duration, accuracy of the lighting and materials that have been assigned, and the image filtering options to determine how accurate the rendering will be.

Once you have finished setting the rendering options, click **Render** to render the image. The Render Output window opens with the rendered image, as shown in Figure 3–11.

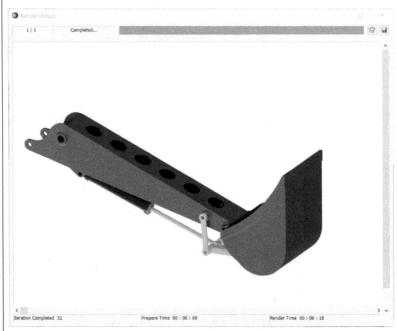

Figure 3–11

Step 6 - Save the image.

If you did not already specify to save the rendered image using the *Output* tab, click 💾 in the Render Output window.

3.2 Animation

Animations can be used to show any of the following:

- Ranges of motion.

- How a model functions.

- How an assembly is assembled.

- How an assembly can be divided into its individual parts or subassemblies.

- How parts in an assembly interact with one another, as well as with external components.

General Steps

Use the following general steps to animate an assembly:

1. Position the components.
2. Define appearance and lighting styles.
3. Define the animation actions.
4. Animate cameras.
5. Render the animation.

Step 1 - Position the components.

Position the components in their required starting positions by adjusting the constraints and/or moving the components.

Step 2 - Define appearance and lighting styles.

Ensure that the required appearances and lighting styles have all been created in the model.

Step 3 - Define the animation actions.

To define the animation actions, start by selecting one of the animate options described as follows from the Animate panel.

(Components)	Animates the position and rotation of components
(Fade)	Animates the visibility of components
(Constraints)	Animates constraint values by specifying an end value
(Parameters)	Animates parameter values, which can be tied to model dimensions
(Pos Reps)	Animates the assembly so that it starts or ends with a Positional Representation
(Light)	Animates the definition of Local Lights including on/off and position

Each animation command dialog box varies, but the common icons are described as follows:

	Starts the action at the time the previous action ended
	Specifies the time to begin the action
	Performs the action instantaneously (in one frame)
	Start time
	Duration
	End time

The *Acceleration* tab, as shown in Figure 3–12, is common among all animation command dialog boxes. It controls the speed of an action as it reaches its target and the percentage of time/actual time for an action to reach its speed and wind down.

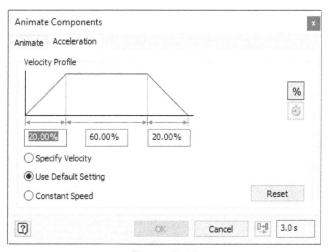

Figure 3–12

Animate Components

The Animate Components dialog box is shown in Figure 3–13. With (Components) toggled on, select one or more components to move or rotate. Click (Position) and the 3D Move/Rotate dialog box opens, enabling you to move or rotate the component(s) in the direction of a free degree of freedom. Enter *Distance* and *Rotation* values as required, and specify a smooth or straight path of motion.

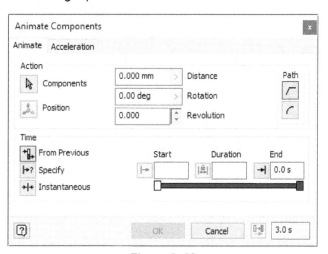

Figure 3–13

Animate Fade

The Animate Fade dialog box is shown in Figure 3–14. With

(Components) toggled on, select one or more components you want to animate. Use the value field to specify the visibility of the selected component(s). To return a component to the previous visibility state at a later time, create another action.

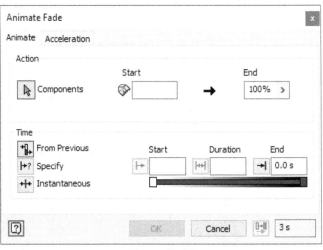

Figure 3–14

Animate Constraints

The Animate Constraints dialog box is shown in Figure 3–15. With (Select) toggled on, select one or more constraints you want to manipulate. To animate a change in a linear or angular constraint value, click $d0=$ (Constraint) and enter the end value. Note that the initial value for the constraint is automatically obtained from the assembly. Click (Suppress) to suppress a constraint or (Enable) to enable a constraint.

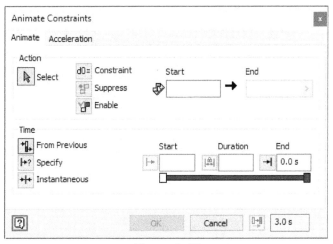

Figure 3–15

Animate Parameters

The Animate Parameters dialog box is shown in Figure 3–16.

With 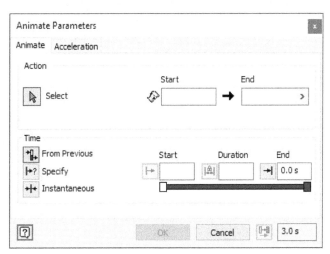 (Select) toggled on, select a parameter you want to manipulate in the *Animation Favorites* area of the Model Browser. The value of the selected parameter is automatically obtained from the model. Specify an end value for the parameter.

Only parameters that have been designated for export and then marked as a favorite

using f_x (Parameter Favorites) are available for use in an animation.

Figure 3–16

Animate Positional Representations

The Animate Positional Representations dialog box is shown in Figure 3–17. Select the start and end Positional Representation positions for the animation. The Positional Representations must already exist in the model to be available in the Start and End drop-down lists.

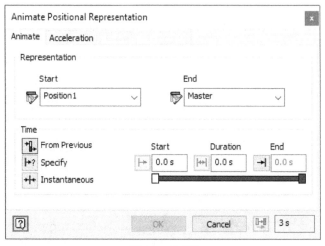

Figure 3–17

Animate Light

The Animate Light dialog box is shown in Figure 3–18. Click

(Select) and select a local light you want to manipulate. Click

(Definition) to open the Local Lights dialog box to change the light information.

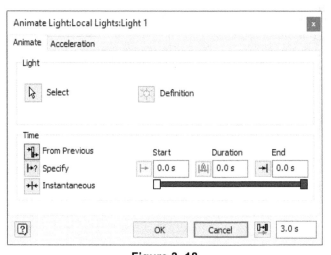

Figure 3–18

Animation Timeline

When working with any of the animation dialog boxes, such as Animate Components or Animate Constraints, the Animation Timeline dialog box opens, as shown in Figure 3–19.

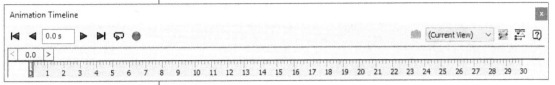

Figure 3–19

To open the Animation Timeline independently of the animate commands, click

(Animation Timeline) in the Animate panel.

Use the animation timeline to control the current time in seconds. The available icons are described as follows:

Icon	Description
◄◄	Sets the current time to the beginning of the animation where the time is zero seconds
◄	Plays the animation in reverse
►	Plays the animation
►►	Sets the current time to the end of the animation
⟳	Toggles between repeating and not repeating the animation
●	Opens the Render Animation dialog box
📷	Creates a camera action that ends at the current time
	Opens the Animation Options dialog box and enables you to specify the duration of the animation in minutes and seconds. Click to fit the length of the animation to the current time.
	Expands the actions editor, as shown below. Actions are listed on the left side, while their start, duration, and end times are represented on the right side. Use this dialog box to view, edit, and delete existing actions. Edit or delete an action by right-clicking on the required action duration bar and selecting **Edit** or **Delete**. You can also adjust the durations of actions directly by dragging the duration bars.

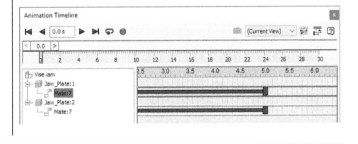

Step 4 - Animate cameras.

In the Animate panel, click 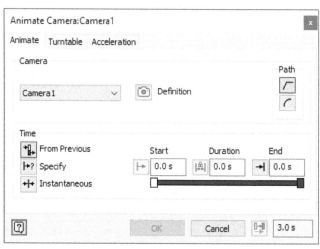 (Camera). The Animate Camera dialog box opens, as shown in Figure 3–20.

Figure 3–20

To define a new camera, click

(Camera) in the Scene panel before opening the Animate Camera dialog box.

Select a camera that has already been defined from the Camera drop-down list and select the path type. The *Path* area provides options to define the camera motion smoothly between the *Start*, *Duration*, and *End* timing values or to define the motion sharply with no smoothing. Click (Definition) to specify the end position of the camera and its target.

Step 5 - Render the animation.

In the Render panel, click 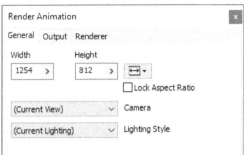 (Render Animation) to open the Render Animation dialog box, as shown in Figure 3–21.

Figure 3–21

General Tab

In the *General* tab, specify the required width and height as well as the specific camera and lighting style.

Output Tab

In the *Output* tab, you can specify the animation's:

- Name and directory

- Time range to record

- Format (save as a video or individual image files)

- Frame rate

Changing the time range increases or decreases the amount of the animation that is recorded in the video file. Alternatively, increasing the frame rate increases the number of frames captured per second. This increases the total number of frames that are animated, which increases the time it takes to create the animation. The benefit of increasing the frame rate, however, is that the animation displays smoother.

- Use the **Preview: No Render** option to preview the animation without rendering the model. This is useful if you only want the animation without rendering.

- The **Launch Player** option plays the newly created animation immediately after it is created.

Renderer Tab

In the *Renderer* tab, you can control the:

- Render duration,

- Accuracy of the lighting and materials that have been assigned, and

- The image filtering option, which determines the accuracy of the rendering.

After selecting the required options from the three tabs, click **Render.** Next, specify the video compression and click **OK** to begin the rendering. Once the rendering has finished, you can go to the folder in which you created the animation and double-click on it to play it. If you enabled the **Launch Player** option, it automatically plays for you.

3.3 Video Producer

The Video Producer enables you to combine camera shots, animations, and transitions into a composite video. To create a video using the Video Producer, simply drag and drop camera shots or transitions from the browser into the timeline. The Video Producer is shown in Figure 3–22.

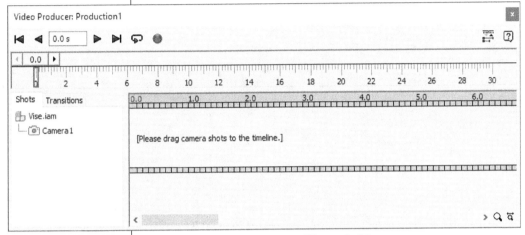

Figure 3–22

General Steps

Use the following general steps to animate an assembly:

1. Create cameras and animations.
2. Display the Video Producer.
3. Add cameras to the production.
4. Add transitions to the production.
5. Arrange cameras and transitions and set the times for both.
6. Render the production.

Step 1 - Create cameras and animations.

Set up the required cameras and animations in Inventor Studio that is going to be used to produce your video.

Step 2 - Display the Video Producer.

In the Animate panel, click ![clapperboard icon] (Video Producer) to open the Video Producer dialog box. This dialog box is used to combine and configure the animations for the video. The various areas of the Video Producer dialog box are shown in Figure 3–23.

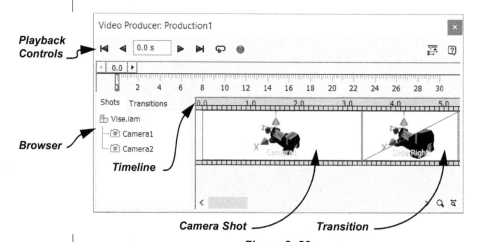

Figure 3–23

The areas of the Video Producer dialog box are described as follows:

Playback Controls	These are the same controls that are present in the Animation Timeline dialog box.
Browser	The Browser contains a *Shots* tab and a *Transitions* tab. The *Shots* tab is automatically populated with cameras that were created in Inventor Studio.
Timeline	Add camera shots and transitions to the timeline and arrange them in the order in which they display in the video.
Camera Shot	Add camera shots to the timeline to display animations of the assembly.
Transition	Add transitions to create effects between camera shots.

- The combination of camera shots and transitions is referred to as a *production*. Each production that you create is listed in the Browser.

Step 3 - Add cameras to the production.

To add cameras to the production, right-click and select **Add to timeline** or drag and drop from the Shots Browser, as shown in Figure 3–24. After the cameras are added to the production, you can edit them to change the duration of the shot and the animation assigned.

Drag cameras and transitions from here

Drag cameras and transitions to here

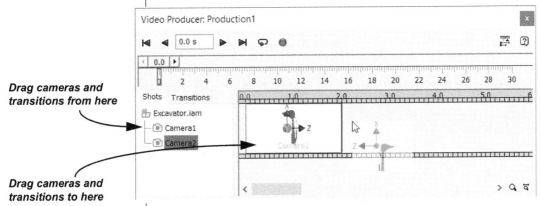

Figure 3–24

Step 4 - Add transitions to the production.

In the *Transitions* tab, you can add transitions between camera shots to create different effects. Standard options include **Fade**, **Gradient Wipe**, **Slide Left**, and **Slide Right**. Right-click and select **Add to timeline** or drag and drop from the Browser to add it to the production, as shown in Figure 3–25. After a transition is added, you can edit it to modify its duration, color, and type.

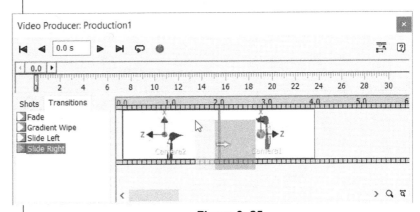

Figure 3–25

Step 5 - Arrange cameras and transitions and set the times for both.

After cameras and transitions are added to the production, they can be modified to further enhance the video. You can modify cameras and transitions by dragging and dropping or using the shortcut menu.

- Click and drop an object in the timeline window to change the sequence of the video. Click and drag the edge of an object to change the duration, as shown in Figure 3–26.

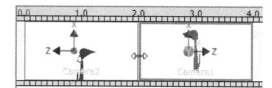

Figure 3–26

- Cameras and transitions can also be modified using the shortcut menu. Right-click options include **Copy**, **Paste**, **Edit**, **Move**, and **Delete**. When you edit a camera, the Shot dialog box opens, as shown in Figure 3–27. You can assign an animation to the shot and set the start point in that animation in the *Animation Footage* area. Assign the camera, duration, and end time in the *Shot Footage* area.

Figure 3–27

When you edit a transition, the Effect dialog box opens, as shown in Figure 3–28. Set the required effect in the *Transition* area, the color in the *Color* area, and the time in the *Timeline position* area.

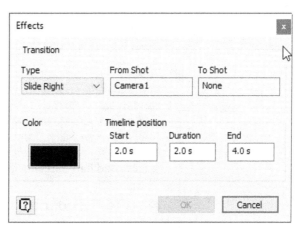

Figure 3–28

Step 6 - Render the production.

Click ● (Record Animation) in the Animation Timeline to open the Render Animation dialog box. This is the same dialog box that is used to render animations.

3.4 Creating a Standard Room

To make the model environment more realistic, you can add walls, a floor, and other relevant objects, such as a table. Because a scene style only adds a background, you need to create the walls, a floor, and other objects, and then assemble them into an assembly to complete the overall environment.

To speed up the process of future renderings, create a new standard assembly you can use for your most common renderings. This might include a left wall, right wall, back wall, and a floor. Create each wall as a separate component to ensure maximum flexibility. For example, different models are likely to be different sizes. Therefore, you want your standard room to be easily modifiable to fit any model size.

How To: Render a Model

1. Create a new assembly.
2. Add the standard room assembly containing the walls and floor.
3. Assemble the model.

By assembling both the standard room and the model into a top-level assembly, you can change the environment quickly and easily. You can also disable the visibility of specific walls and other objects, as required.

For the floor and each wall, you can apply a different appearance to achieve the required result.

Practice 3a

Rendering Images and an Animation

Practice Objectives

- Apply an Appearance Override to individual parts in an assembly.
- Apply a lighting style to a model.
- Create a realistic rendered image and animation.

In this practice, you will apply appearance overrides and a lighting style to an assembly model for rendering both an image and animation. The image shown in Figure 3–29 is one of the images that you will create.

Figure 3–29

Task 1 - Open an assembly file and apply appearance overrides.

1. Open **Vise.iam** from the *Vise_Inv_Studio_Assembly* folder.

2. In the Model Browser, select the **Screw_Sub:1** subassembly.

3. In the Quick Access toolbar, click (Appearance) to open the Appearance Browser.

4. In the Appearance Browser, enter **Chrome** in the *Search* field at the top of the dialog box.

5. In the search results, select **Chrome - Polished**, and then right-click on it and select **Assign to Selection**. The material on the subassembly is now overridden and the Chrome - Polished material is now listed in the *Document Appearances* area.

6. Clear the *Search* field entry.

7. Clear the selection of the subassembly and in the Model Browser, select **Sliding_Jaw** and **Base**.

8. Scroll down the list of materials in the Inventor Materials Library and select the **Metal** option. Right-click on **Metal 1400F Hot**, and then select **Assign to Selection**. This material is assigned to the model and is copied to the *Document Appearances* area of the dialog box.

9. Close the Appearance Browser.

Task 2 - Set up the ground plane and set reflections.

1. In the *View* tab>Appearance panel, click **Ground Plane** to enable and display the ground plane in the graphics window.

2. Click **Front** on the ViewCube. Note how the model is sitting on the ground plane. This should be verified to ensure that any reflections that are used when rendering are accurate.

3. Click **Ground Plane** to disable its display. The ground plane was only required to ensure that the reflections are correctly rendered.

4. Using the ViewCube return the model to the **Home** view.

5. In the *View* tab>Appearance panel, click **Reflections** to enable it. A reflection is displayed in the graphics window.

*To adjust the ground plane location, expand **Ground Plane** in the Appearance panel and click **Settings**. In the Ground Plane Settings dialog box, ensure that the **Automatic adjustment to model** option is selected and enter a value in the Position & Size area to better position the plane.*

Task 3 - Open the Inventor Studio Environment.

1. In the *Environments* tab>Begin panel, click (Inventor Studio). The *Render* contextual tab displays.

2. The rendering will be the size of the graphics window. Zoom the model as required so that it uses the full size of the window.

3. In the Render panel, click (Render Image). The Render Image dialog box opens, as shown in Figure 3–30. By default, the current view and lighting is used for rendering.

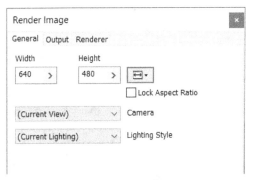

Figure 3–30

4. Expand the Lighting Style drop-down list and select **Cool Light**.

5. Expand the drop-down list and select **Active View**. This sets the size of the rendered image to that of the current graphics window.

6. Select the *Renderer* tab. Change *Render Duration* to **Until Satisfactory** and leave the remaining defaults in the dialog box.

7. Click **Render**. Note the background in the rendering is still white. This is because the scene image is not displayed.

   Click (Stop Rendering) in the top right-hand corner of the dialog box and close the Render Output dialog box.

8. In the Scene panel, click (Studio Lighting Styles). The Studio Lighting Styles dialog box opens. Note that **Cool Light** is the active style.

9. In the *Environment* tab, click **Display Scene Image** to enable it and click **Save**.

   - You cannot enable the scene image when assigning the lighting style in the Render Image dialog box. The image is only rendered with the lighting effects of the image.

10. Click **Done** to close the Studio Lighting Styles dialog box. Note that the background now displays as gray. This is the background image for the cool light environment.

11. In the Render panel, click  (Render Image) again. Verify that **Cool Light** is set as the *Lighting Style* and the render duration (*Renderer* tab) is set to render until satisfactory.

12. Click **Render**. The render will continue until you click (Stop Rendering). The longer you let the image render, the better the rendering quality.

To automatically save an image once rendered, use the options on the Output tab.

13. Once the image is rendered, click (Save Rendering) in the Render Output window. In the Save dialog box, navigate to the *Vise_Inv_Studio_Assembly* folder and enter **Vise_Rendering1.bmp** as the name. Click **Save**. The model shown in Figure 3–31 was rendered for over ten minutes.

Figure 3–31

14. Close the Render Output dialog box.

15. On the *General* tab, in the Lighting Style drop-down list, select **Sharp Highlights**. Return to the Studio Lighting Styles dialog box and ensure that the **Display Scene Image** is enabled.

16. In the Render Image dialog box, render the image. After approximately ten minutes it should display similar to that shown in Figure 3–32. Save it as **Vise_Rendering2.bmp**.

Figure 3–32

17. Close the Render Output and Render Image dialog boxes.

*If you did not complete the two renderings, two images (**Vise_ Rendering1_Final.bmp** and **Vise_Rendering2 _Final.bmp**) are provided in the Vise_ Inv_Studio_Assembly folder for you to compare.*

18. Navigate to the *Vise_Inv_Studio_Assembly* folder in Windows Explorer and open the two saved images (**Vise_Rendering1.bmp** and **Vise_Rendering2.bmp**) to compare them. Note that the lighting in the second image is considerably brighter. This is because of the different image-based lighting style that was used. You will want to compare different styles to select the one that is best for your designs.

Task 4 - Working with a lighting style.

1. In the Scene panel, click ✎ (Studio Lighting Styles). The Studio Lighting Styles dialog box opens, as shown in Figure 3–33.

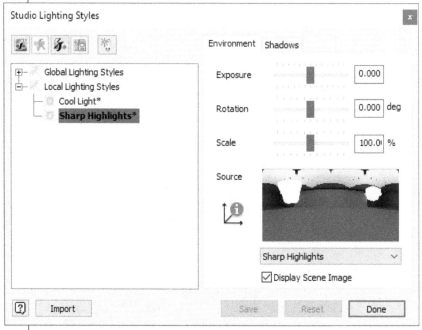

Figure 3–33

2. The **Cool Light** and **Sharp Highlights** styles have been copied to the Local Lighting Styles area because they were used for rendering. They can be further edited using the options, as required.

3. Right-click on **Cool Light** and note all of the options that you can select. The style can be renamed, copied, or deleted (purged), as required.

4. Select **Rename Lighting Style** and enter **Custom Lighting** as the new name and then click **OK**.

5. Locate the **Empty Lab** style in the *Global Lighting Styles* area. Right-click on the style, select **Copy Lighting Style**, and then enter a new name. The new style is listed in the **Local Lighting Styles** node.

6. Set the new style as **Active**, if not already set.

7. Select **Display Scene Image** to show the style's background image in the graphics window.

8. Scale the background image to match the size of the model (approx. 36%).

9. Rotate the environment and the model, as required.

10. In the *View* tab, toggle off reflections and toggle on ground shadows.

11. Save the style and render the model.

A rendered version of the model is shown in Figure 3–34. **Vise_Rendering3_Final.bmp** has been saved for you to review in the *Vise_Inv_Studio_Assembly* folder, if required.

Figure 3–34

12. Close the Render Output and Render Image dialog boxes.

Task 5 - Create an animation for the opening of the jaw plates.

1. In the Scene panel, click 🔅 (Studio Lighting Styles).

2. Activate the **Custom Lighting** style that was previously created. Close the Studio Lighting Styles dialog box.

3. Return to the model's **Home** view.

4. Select the *View* tab and disable the display of shadows in the animation. Enabling shadows in this video does not produce a good result because of the movement of the shadows throughout the video.

5. In the *Render* tab>Animate panel, click 🎞 (Constraints). Click **OK** if prompted to activate an animation. The Animate Constraints dialog box (shown in Figure 3–35) and the Animation Timeline opens.

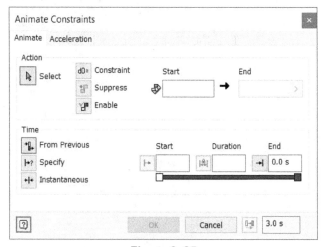

Figure 3–35

6. In the Model Browser, expand the **Jaw_Plate:1** branch and select **Mate:7** as the constraint to animate.

7. Type **65 mm** as the *End* constraint value and **5.0 s** as the *End* time value, as shown in Figure 3–36.

If required, specify a duration longer than 5.0 s to view a smoother animation.

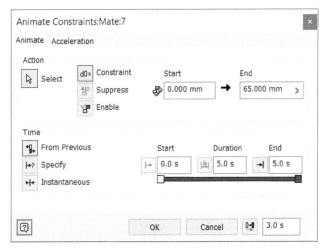

Figure 3–36

8. Click **OK** to complete the definition.

9. Click (Expand Action Editor) in the Animation Timeline window to expand the window, as shown in Figure 3–37.

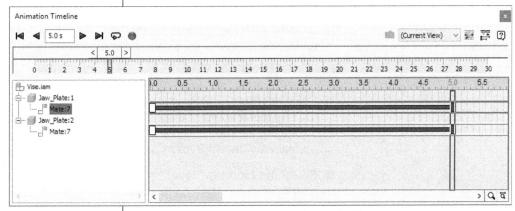

Figure 3–37

10. The animated Mate constraint you added earlier is in the animation timeline. The blue bar indicates the duration of the motion. By default, the total animation time is 30s. Change the total time to 5s by clicking (Animation Options) and typing **5** in the *Seconds* field. Click **OK** to confirm and close the Animation Options dialog box.

11. In the Animation Timeline window, click (Go to Start) to set the animation to the beginning. The model returns to its initial state.

12. Run the animation by clicking ▶ (Play Animation).

13. Refit and orient the model in the window, as required, to render the animation.

14. In the Render panel, click 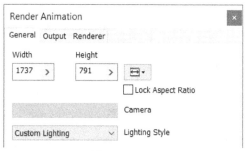 (Render Animation). The Render Animation dialog box opens, as shown in Figure 3–38.

Figure 3–38

15. Expand the ⊡▾ drop-down list and select **Active View**. This sets the size of the rendered animation to that of the graphics window.

16. Select the *Output* tab and set the *Vise_Inv_Studio_Assembly* folder and file name for the animation. Use the default .WMV file format. Click **Save**.

17. Click ⊞ (Specified Time Range) and type **2.0s** to animate for only this amount of time. This reduces the time it takes to create the animation, but also only records half of the total animation. Therefore, the vise will not completely open.

18. Select the **Launch Player** option to automatically play the animation once it has been created.

19. Select the *Renderer* tab. Select **Total Render Time**. Note that the default rendering time is 1 min. Maintain this default, noting that rendering for longer creates better results.

20. Click **Render**.

21. In the ASF Export Properties dialog box, keep the default settings and click **OK**. (If you saved as an .AVI file, the Video Compression dialog box opens.) The rendering will begin.

22. View the animation when it displays.

23. Save the model and close the window.

Practice 3b

Puncher

Practice Objectives

- Create a room to provide an environment for models to use for their renderings.
- Modify appearances and lighting styles to render an image.

In this practice, you will create a room that future models can use for their renderings. You will use this room to provide an environment for the rendering of the puncher assembly, shown in Figure 3–39. General instructions are provided.

Figure 3–39

Task 1 - Create a new empty assembly and add walls and puncher assembly.

---

1. Open **Puncher.iam** from the *Inventor Studio - Puncher* folder.

2. Create a new metric part called **Floor** outside of this assembly. This part will provide a surface on which the Puncher assembly will rest. The part can be a large thin rectangular block. You can make the block much larger than the Puncher assembly. Add dimensions to make it easier to modify later on. For your reference, the puncher assembly is approximately 144 mm wide, 202 mm long, and 160 mm tall. This part will simulate the surface of a table in the rendering.

3. Create another new metric part called **Back_Wall** outside of the Puncher assembly to act as a back wall in the rendering. Make this part a thin rectangular block as well, and then add dimensions to it.

Once rooms have been created once, they are ready to use in future renderings. You can save them in a library for use by other designers.

4. Create a third part, called **Left_Wall**, to act as the left wall in the rendering. This will be another thin rectangular block. Add dimensions to the part.

5. Create a fourth part called **Right_Wall**.

6. Create a new empty assembly and assemble **Floor.ipt**, **Back_ Wall.ipt**, **Left_Wall.ipt**, and **Right_Wall.ipt**.

7. Save the assembly and call it **Room1**.

8. Create another new empty assembly and place Room1 as the first component.

9. Place the Puncher assembly and position it in the middle of the room.

10. Modify the dimensions of any of the walls to suit the Puncher assembly.

11. Save the assembly and call it **Room_Puncher**.

12. Apply appearances to the back wall, side wall, and floor using the Appearance Browser.

13. Switch to Inventor Studio.

14. Select an existing or create a new lighting style.

15. Zoom in on the room so that only the room's walls display in the graphics window. If not, once rendered the background that was assigned to the lighting style will be displayed in the rendering.

16. Render the image and select the required resolution and lighting styles.

17. Save the rendered image.

18. If you did not achieve your required result, modify the appearances and lighting styles to work as required. Render the assembly again.

19. Continue to modify the appearances and styles until you obtain your required result.

20. Save and close the assembly when you are finished.

Practice 3c

Excavator

Practice Objective

- Create a rendered animation of an assembly.

In this practice, you will create an animation for the excavator assembly shown in Figure 3–40. General instructions are provided.

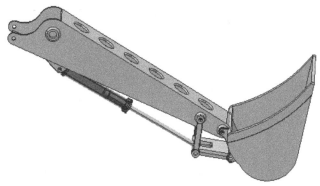

Figure 3–40.

Task 1 - Create an animated rendering of an assembly.

1. Open **Excavator_complete.iam** from the *Inventor Studio-Excavator* folder.

2. Create an animation for the assembly. Animate **Mate:20**, which is located in the *Cylinder* subassembly.
    - Specify an End value of **1500 mm**.
    - Specify an appropriate duration for the action so that it will not take too long to create an animation for it.
    - Adjust the length of the animation using the animation options on the Animation Timeline window.
    - Preview the animation using the Animation Timeline window and make adjustments as required.

3. Open the Render Animation dialog box and enter the required options in the *General*, *Output*, and *Renderer* tabs. Adjust the frame rate and time range to reduce the time it will take to create the animation.

4. Render the animation. While the animation process is running, check the total number of frames that need to be created. If the number of frames is too high and you estimate that the process will take too long, stop the animation and adjust the rendering options in the *Output* tab. Rerun the rendering as required.

5. To add additional detail to the rendered animation, consider using a lighting style with a background image (e.g. Old Warehouse) or using the room assembly technique to place the assembly in a room that has had appearances assigned to its walls. Render the animation again.

6. Save and close the assembly.

Chapter Review Questions

1. What is the purpose of Inventor Studio?
   a. Create positional representations of models.
   b. Create a background for models.
   c. Create realistic renderings and animations.

2. What are the three types of lights that can be assigned in a light style?
   a. Spot, Directional, and Cloud.
   b. Spot, Directional, and Shadow.
   c. Point, Directional, and Cloud.
   d. Directional, Spot, and Point.

3. When rendering an image, where do you set the rendering duration to proceed before the action is completed?
   a. Render Image dialog box, *General* tab.
   b. Render Image dialog box, *Output* tab.
   c. Render Image dialog box, *Renderer* tab.

4. Along with animating components, which of the following can also be animated? (Select all that apply.)
   a. Constraints
   b. Parameters
   c. Level of Detail
   d. Cameras
   e. Lights

5. Along with dragging and dropping a camera from the Video Producer to the timeline, how else can you add it to the production?
   a. Click the **Add to Timeline** icon in the ribbon.
   b. Double-click on it in the Video Producer.
   c. Right-click on it and select **Add to Timeline**.
   d. All of the above.

Answers: 1c, 2d, 3c, 4abde, 5c

Command Summary

Button	Command	Location
	Animation Timeline	• **Ribbon:** *Render* tab>Animate panel
	Appearance	• **Ribbon:** *Tools* tab>Material and Appearance panel • **Quick Access Toolbar**
	Camera	• **Ribbon:** *Render* tab>Scene panel
	Camera (animate)	• **Ribbon:** *Render* tab>Animate panel
	Clear	• **Ribbon:** *Tools* tab>Material and Appearance panel • **Quick Access Toolbar**
	Components	• **Ribbon:** *Render* tab>Animate panel
	Constraints	• **Ribbon:** *Render* tab>Animate panel
	Fade	• **Ribbon:** *Render* tab>Animate panel
	Inventor Studio	• **Ribbon:** *Environments* tab>Begin panel
	Light	• **Ribbon:** *Render* tab>Animate panel
	Local Lights	• **Ribbon:** *Render* tab>Scene panel
fx	**Parameter Favorites**	• **Ribbon:** *Render* tab>Animate panel
	Parameters	• **Ribbon:** *Render* tab>Animate panel
	Pos Reps	• **Ribbon:** *Render* tab>Manage panel
	Render Animation	• **Ribbon:** *Render* tab>Render panel
	Render Image	• **Ribbon:** *Render* tab>Render panel
	Studio Lighting Styles	• **Ribbon:** *Render* tab>Scene panel
	Video Producer	• **Ribbon:** *Render* tab>Animate panel

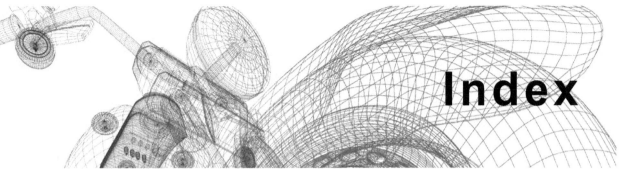

Index

www.ingramcontent.com/pod-product-compliance
Lightning Source LLC
LaVergne TN
LVHW080059070326

832902LV00014B/2313

* 9 7 8 1 9 5 2 8 6 6 3 6 4 *